Leslie Watkins is a [illegible] in many leading pu[illegible] the *Sunday Times* [illegible] *The Sleepwalk* [illegible] somnambulistic vi[illegible] first novel, *The Kill*[illegible] he was in prison in Uganda – having been arrested by Amin's men as a suspected spy after arriving in the country as a correspondent for the *Daily Mail.* Subsequently he has written two more novels, *The Unexploded Man* and *Alternative 3.*

Mr Watkins lives in Devon.

The Real Exorcists

Leslie Watkins

Futura

A Futura Book

First published in Great Britain in 1983
by Metheun London Ltd

This edition published in 1984
by Futura Publications, a Division of
Macdonald & Co (Publishers) Ltd
London & Sydney

ISBN 0 7088 2586 9

Printed and bound in Great Britain by
Collins, Glasgow

Futura Publications
A Division of
Macdonald & Co (Publishers) Ltd
Maxwell House
74 Worship Street
London EC2A 2EN

A BPCC plc Company

Contents

1	Epidemic of demons	7
2	Confronting black magic	31
3	Manipulators of evil?	43
4	Ouija	53
5	Intruders from the grave	73
6	The distinctive smell of evil	94
7	Controversy in the medical profession	106
8	Religious fanaticism in America	126
9	Religious fanaticism in Britain	141
10	Controversy within the churches	156
11	Is the Bible wrong about exorcism and demons?	172
12	Is there a genuine need for exorcism?	179
	Index	187

AUTHOR'S NOTE

Throughout this book certain names have been changed in order to protect the privacy of the families and individuals concerned. Names which have been changed are indicated by an asterisk.

1 Epidemic of demons

Some frightened and tormented person is almost certainly being exorcised at this moment – as you read these words – for dozens of these ceremonies are performed every day in Britain. Some take several hours. Others last only minutes. They are conducted by priests and by lay preachers, by spiritualists and by self-proclaimed witches or magicians. Some ceremonies are arranged at the request of psychiatrists and family doctors, for there is a growing conviction in the medical profession that many problems, which might seem to stem from some mental affliction, can be caused by invisible forces of evil. This is why exorcisms have been performed discreetly in the surgeries of general practitioners and even in a hospital run by the National Health Service. This is also why there is a lobby for exorcism to be recognised officially as an additional type of treatment in special hospitals such as Broadmoor.

'Exorcism' comes from the Greek *exousia*, meaning 'to dismiss'. It is now causing bitter divisions within the churches. Many religious leaders dismiss the concept of possession as an embarrassing and potentially dangerous legacy of our ancient superstitions. Others are convinced that alien spirits can create havoc by trespassing into homes or human bodies. There are also fundamentalists who see all sicknesses, set-backs and sorrows as the work of demons.

While this controversy simmers, however, the exorcists are increasingly busy. Devil-worship is more rampant throughout the civilised world than at any time since the Middle Ages. So is dabbling in witchcraft and in other aspects of the occult such as party-game attempts to summon the spirits of the dead. This has helped generate a mounting dread of demons and other baleful entities. Despite the sophisticated advances in science, vast numbers of intelligent and highly educated people accept the possibility of psychic invasion.

Father Ian Hazlewood is the Church of England's official exorcist in the Diocese of Gloucester. Cases are often referred to him by a doctor, who considers that a high percentage of patients' problems are spiritual rather than medical, and he averages one or two exorcisms a week.

In July 1981 he told me: 'During the last two years, and the last twelve months in particular, there has been an increasing demand for this type of help.' Other experienced and respected exorcists in many parts of the country confirmed this growth. What was causing it?

Father Hazlewood believes that 'The growth in materialism is making people feel a deep need for spiritual truths, possibly more than ever before, and they are simply not finding them in their local churches. The churches, in fact, are failing them – and failing to fulfil the commission given by Christ. So more and more people, especially youngsters, are attracted towards psychic experimentation. This means they are exposing themselves to great dangers – which should never be underestimated – and are likely to eventually need cleansing through exorcism.'

However, the need for such 'cleansing' – if it exists at all – is often difficult to identify. Many exorcists concede that one of their fundamental problems is that of diagnosis. Hysteria? Mental sickness? A possessing entity so devious that it can create an illusion of these conditions – as a confusing camouflage which enables it to remain undetected?

Symptoms which may seem obvious can be misleading, for medical men as well as priests, and this could explain why many exorcisms end in apparent failure.

Keith* is a married man who lives in Somerset. For six years psychiatrists tried to relieve his emotional difficulties, which he insisted were being caused by an alien spirit of violence. They were unsuccessful. They had described him in their notes as a potentially aggressive neurotic and given him tranquillisers. Finally they considered there was nothing more they could do. That was when he asked for exorcism. In August 1981 four casting-out ceremonies were performed by Father John Wheaton at the Oratory of Our Lady in Exeter. Father Wheaton is a priest in the Liberal Catholic Church. This is an autonomous church which, like certain other Catholic churches such as the Greek Orthodox and the Coptic, is independent of Rome. Its Holy Orders were derived from the Old Catholic Church of Holland and it is a constituent part of the One Holy Catholic and Apostolic Church.

The exorcisms were not successful and it was then decided to seek additional help – that of another Liberal Catholic, a veteran clairvoyant, Father Arnold Clare. Maybe he could establish whether Keith was the victim of possession or of some clinical condition.

My first meeting with Keith was oddly disconcerting. He beamed with pleasure and claimed to recognise me instantly because he had seen me regularly in visions. 'I often have visions of people who are going to come into my life,' he said. Then he frowned, as if puzzled, and stared at my face. 'But there's something different about you today. You should be wearing spectacles – funny, half-moon ones with a flat-topped frame – because that's how you've always appeared.'

We had never met before and, to the best of my knowledge, he had never seen me before. I produced my reading-glasses from their case which was in my inside pocket. They were exactly as he'd described them. 'Ah yes . . . they're the ones,' he said calmly. 'You're always wearing them in the visions.' Within minutes he was telling me about myself, describing details of my background and my family which he could not normally have known and which were certainly not known by Father Wheaton. He spoke with accuracy about my parents and my childhood.

This information, given spontaneously in the presence of Father Wheaton, must have reached Keith through telepathy. There was no other logical explanation. Yet it was telepathy at a highly-developed level for at that time I was concentrating on him, observing and assessing him, and I was certainly not thinking of the facts he was giving so accurately.

'There's no need to be surprised,' he said. 'You're seeing me as a stranger but I've known you well for a long time.' He paused. 'Have you got an old-fashioned spinning-wheel?' I shook my head. 'That's curious,' he said. 'I've often seen you sitting beside one of those old spinning-wheels. You and it being together – that's the way it ought to be. Are you *sure* there isn't one at your home?'

'Absolutely certain.'

He studied me carefully as if wondering if I was telling the truth. 'I've had clear visions of you sitting beside it,' he persisted. 'And I know that in some way that's tied in with me being helped. . . '

He had been having visions, he claimed, ever since he was a small child. 'And I'm not talking about dreams,' he added. 'I'm talking about people and things that come to me when I'm wide awake – sometimes in the middle of the day – and stay for a while before suddenly disappearing. Some of them are monstrous things, huge and black and obscene, which taunt me and try to goad me into awful violence.'

There were just the three of us – Father Wheaton, myself and this curious but patently sincere man – in a small sitting-room near the oratory.

'I also have visions of myself as I was in an earlier life,' he said. 'I was here in England hundreds of years ago and I was a witch-hunter. I was very powerful then and also very cruel. I enjoyed persecuting people and having them tortured. But men I thought were my friends betrayed me and I was killed in the most agonising way. I've seen myself very clearly being drawn and quartered and I knew that I deserved it. I'd done things that were terrible and wicked. And the evil that was in me then is still inside me today.'

He patted the lower part of his chest. 'I can feel it distinctly as something quite separate from me. It's difficult to describe in physical terms but the best I can say is that it's like having a balloon inside me.'

This 'something of evil', he claimed, often tried to force him into acts of violence or destruction. 'It urges me to lash out at people or to wreck things. It tries to persuade me to injure myself. If I'm peeling potatoes, for instance, it keeps telling me destruction there, but then paused to sneer at Father Wheaton: 'You've lost, priest! You with your idiot prattling. . . you've been wasting your time. . .'

Father Wheaton swallowed hard and then, speaking with quiet authority, began moving slowly towards him: 'You'd better come over here and sit down. . .'

'Get back!' Keith clenched his fists and began flexing his shoulders like a wrestler. 'Keep away, priest, or I'll cripple you. . .'

Before being ordained Father Wheaton was a policeman in London. He'd had to deal with many threats of violence. Now he was maintaining an air of unruffled calm. His outstretched arms were wide apart, as if he was ready to embrace Keith, and he was still moving closer.

Keith suddenly lowered his head in shamed despair and his fury was replaced by remorse. His body sagged, as if in great weariness, and all the menace had now drained away.

'I'm sorry. . . I really am sorry. . .' Tears were welling in his eyes and his distress seemed genuine. 'I know what I said, but, please believe me, it wasn't me saying it. . .'

He sat meekly while Father Wheaton, standing behind him, gently cradled his head and prayed. He continued to apologise when we retired to the nearby room.

'I don't want to seem rude but, let's face it, you're not getting anywhere,' he said eventually. 'There seems no point in you trying any more.'

Was he really possessed by a spirit of evil? Or did his problems stem from a condition which was purely medical or emotional? I put those questions privately to Father Wheaton. 'Quite frankly, I don't know,' he admitted. 'I'm as baffled as the psychiatrists. All I do know is that he needs some sort of help.'

It was agreed to seek the advice of Father Clare. The hope was that clairvoyance would produce a diagnosis.

The word 'clairvoyance' comes from the French *clair* meaning 'clear' and *voir*, to see. It relates to the power of seeing things not normally perceptible to the senses and is more commonly known as second sight.

The predominant attitude to it in the mainstream churches

tends to be one of suspicion. Many religious leaders dismiss it as an activity for cranks or charlatans. But there is a conflict of opinions. Some of the exorcists who have been officially appointed as specialists within the Church of England often work in partnership with clairvoyants. They prefer to call them 'Christian psychics'. They respect the guidance given by these people but, fearing the disapproval of their superiors and congregations, they usually consult them in secret. One highly regarded Church of England exorcist told me: 'I have a sensitive who occasionally helps me in difficult cases by passing on information from a dead priest. My bishop doesn't know about this for I feel certain he would not approve. But I am able to help certain people more effectively this way and surely that's what is really important.'

Father Wheaton has a similar respect for 'psychic guidance'.

On 23 August we drove with Keith to the Devon home of Father Clare who, during the previous two days, had been praying for guidance. He questioned Keith briefly before taking us to his own small chapel where, using holy water and incense, he performed a short ceremony of exorcism – similar to those conducted by Father Wheaton. He later explained that this was little more than an 'antiseptic precaution' for he had been convinced, within minutes of meeting Keith, that this was not a case of possession. He had been mentally tuning into Keith during their talk, concentrating more on his mannerisms and his 'vibrations' rather than his words, and he had been satisfied that Keith's problems were caused by a 'psychic or emotional bottleneck'.

'This young man had been trying to develop his own psychic awareness, expanding the powers within him to their utmost limits and he had gone too far too quickly. He didn't have the capability to control these powers, which include that of incipient clairvoyance, and they had formed a blockage which, if it wasn't cleared, would have created far more serious mental instability.'

Father Clare concentrated most of his energies that afternoon into a service of healing, praying as he laid his right hand against the base of Keith's spine. This is the region which, according to esoteric teaching, contains the basic centre known as the *Mulhadara Chakra.* It is regarded as one of the body's psychic 'junction boxes' and in Keith's case, as Father Clare explained, over-stimulation had produced congestion. Father Clare also identified and worked on a similar condition in the Spleen Centre.

Keith had his eyes closed during this service but told me afterwards that he had felt as if he had been 'covered in blue light'. 'There was a wonderful sensation of serenity and I already feel as if I'm different,' he said. 'It's as if that balloon or whatever it was has been taken out of me.' He *looked* different, brighter and more relaxed than I'd ever seen him before. He was also more light-hearted.

While having tea in Father Clare's drawing-room, Keith suddenly pointed to the alcove beside me. It contained an old-fashioned spinning-wheel. 'I knew I was right about you and that spinning-wheel.' Keith's tone was matter-of-fact and calm. 'It was always so clear in my visions.'

This was not an instant 'miracle' cure but merely the beginning of Keith's progress to recovery. Father Clare told me: 'Yes, he's now on the right road but his condition was acute and he's going to need more sessions of healing.'

Within two months, during which he visited Father Clare twice, Keith appeared to be free of his inner turmoil. The outcome was satisfactory although the ceremonies of exorcism had failed. But had they served any useful purpose? That possibility would almost certainly be denied by a number of prominent clerics who, over the past few years, have joined medical men in denouncing all attempts at exorcism.

In 1976 the Reverend Don Cupitt, Dean of Emmanuel College, Cambridge stated in *The Journal of Medical Ethics:*

> The current revival of superstition and spread of religious irrationalism is alarming, not only to men of religion like me, but to men of science also (and to those who are both).
>
> It implies an intellectual regression and a reversion to a more primitive view of the self as a theatre in which opposed supernatural forces battle for supremacy . . .

> The physician's interest is in the restoration of his patient's moral and intellectual health. It would be a dereliction of his duty to encourage the highly obnoxious belief that the self is at the mercy of alien forces – and consequently dependent upon the exorcist or other figure who claims to have the authority to expel evil. There is here the professional man's worst temptation, priestcraft, the spiritual domination of his client.
>
> So, on ethical grounds, I think exorcism should not be performed. On intellectual grounds I think it has no place in modern medicine. And I deplore the suggestion that psychiatrists might recommend certain patients to priests for exorcism. For that proposal suggests an intolerable view of the relations of religion and science.

Keith was not harmed in any way by the exorcisms. He had sought the help of the Church only because of the hope it seemed to offer. This led him to the 'spiritual healing' which, it appears, was more successful than the prolonged efforts of psychiatrists.

* * *

* * *

'Keep away priest, or I'll cripple you . . .'

Warnings of that nature, sometimes followed by violence, are familiar to most exorcists. But more intangible and far more unnerving dangers, they claim, can be unleashed by invisible forces of evil. Exorcists believe that they are regularly confronting Satan, or the emissaries of Satan, and are therefore exposed to counter-attacks by demons. The anticipation of such attacks often fills them with dread.

The Reverend James Song, Vicar of St John's Church, Woking, Surrey testifies to this: 'I have a gift for discerning evil, for knowing when I'm in its presence, and I readily admit that it usually makes me frightened and physically unwell. My temples feel very tight and I nearly always get sudden and severe headaches. Often I have difficulty with my speech.'

The Reverend David MacInnes of Birmingham Cathedral: 'I am aware of a sense of fear which, in a curious way, is almost apart from me. I am detached from it mentally so that it does not impair my thinking or my determination but it takes hold of my physical frame.'

Father Ian Hazlewood of Gloucestershire is a scholarly and reflective man who is anxious to avoid sensationalism. But he insists he was terrified by a singularly powerful demon which possessed a former Guardsman. This young man was in a group which tried a series of experiments in the hope of summoning spirits. Father Hazlewood believes they succeeded in attracting one spirit, an insidiously potent demon, which took possession of the man. From that moment on it controlled his behaviour. It depraved his personality, changed his appearance and came close to devastating his life.

Buildings were mysteriously damaged or gutted by fire and it was established that the demoniac had become an arsonist. He could not give any logical explanation. All he knew was that there was something inside him, something he could not understand, which was driving him to these senseless acts.

Then it was also discovered that he was indulging in homosexual activities, which again seemed curiously out of character, and he was discharged from the army. He returned to his home in Gloucestershire where his mother, appalled by his deterioration, sought the guidance of Father Hazlewood's curate. Late one warm summer evening the curate took him to the vicarage near St Mary's Church, Prestbury, Cheltenham.

'The man looked haggard and far older than his age and there was an unpleasant smell coming from him,' said Father Hazlewood. 'As the three of us sat in my study, the temperature suddenly dropped to zero. It was so cold that we couldn't stop shivering and our teeth, quite literally, were chattering. Confronting someone with true demonic possession is a horrifying experience. The first time I'd done so, some years earlier, I almost fainted and on this occasion my curate and I were both terrified.'

He went to another room to telephone his bishop, the late Right Revd Basil Guy, who immediately gave the authorisation necessary for an exorcism. Then the two clergymen took the demoniac to the church.

Their progress was slow and laborious. It was as if the demon was struggling to exert its will, as thought it was trying to stop them reaching the church. He said, 'Our feet were like lead, almost too heavy to lift, and we could only shuffle along at crawling pace.'

At the communion rail in the high vaulted chancel of the old church, lit only by two candles at the altar, Father Hazlewood sprinkled holy water on the man's head and 'was astonished when it seemed to sizzle'. He persevered, praying and commanding the demon to leave, and then he witnessed an extraordinary change in the man.

He had been kneeling passively at the rail but now he jerked away and, making 'awful animal noises', began crawling around the church. This seemed to be the climax of the demon's defiance, for suddenly the man was still and silent. The entity had gone. In the church, once again, there was tranquillity. The man was restored to normality.

How much credence can be put on the testimony of Father Hazlewood? Is it really conceivable that a discarnate spirit, a malevolent intruder from another sphere, was trying to prevent him reaching his church? Can we accept that contact with the man's head made the holy water 'sizzle'? Or might it not be possible that Father Hazlewood was being deceived by his own emotions or imagination? His evidence, in isolation, might easily be considered suspect. Any serious appraisal of exorcism requires cautious scepticism but that scepticism should be a safeguard rather than a blindfold. Experiences comparable to that related by Father Hazlewood have been described by many exorcists, in a variety of faiths, and by those who have sought their aid. So have ones far more horrendously bizarre. There are too many of these detailed accounts, provided by intelligent people with no apparent motive for exaggeration, for them to be lightly discounted.

* * *
* * *

Former racing-driver Jimmy Gemmell is an evangelist who has a prayer group in Carlisle. He is a burly and phlegmatic character who looks as if he belongs behind a plough rather than in a pulpit. He sometimes performs six or more exorcisms in a week and claims to have been attacked repeatedly by evil.

One such attack occurred in a house near Glasgow where a young man hung himself. His parents were baffled as well as distraught. He had not appeared to be depressed and they were unaware that he had any particular problems. One evening they had left him watching television while they visited friends and he was dead when they returned home. Shortly afterwards they moved. The house was too full of memories. It was bought by a couple with three young children. They knew about the tragedy but were not concerned about spirits or hauntings. Such things were superstitious nonsense.

Troubles began within a week or so of their move. Their six-year-old daughter was seriously injured when she fell down the stairs. The father became repeatedly and unaccountably ill. He lost his job and the marriage began to deteriorate. 'We reached the stage where we were snapping at each other,' he said later. 'Our whole life seemed to have gone sour.' His wife left him. She also abandoned the children, to whom she had been devoted, and for nearly a year he tried to cope with them on his own.

Eventually, in desperation, he contacted Mr Gemmell. 'I know this probably sounds daft . . .' he said apologetically, 'but there is something wrong with this house. There's something bad . . .'

Mr Gemmell, accompanied by two members of his prayer group, advised the father to leave with his children. He then began the exorcism in the front bedroom.

He claims that he can feel the presence of evil and 'that there was just a trace of it, nothing more than that, in the bedroom'. He addressed himself directly to that evil, 'In the name of Jesus Christ, I come against you Satan and demon powers; I bind you in the almighty name of Jesus Christ and I command you to go to the place that the Lord and Saviour has prepared for you – there to await the day of judgement.'

Nothing happened. He gave the same command in the second bedroom and then the third. This is his normal procedure when exorcising a house. He 'cleanses' the upstairs, one room at a time, and then does the same downstairs – 'rather like a woman sweeping through the place with a brush'. There was no apparent reaction in the bedrooms. In the bathroom he expected to find the real core of evil, for that was where the man had been driven to kill himself, and he protected himself with more prayers before stepping in. But he was mistaken. The atmosphere was no worse than in the bedrooms. But a few minutes later he felt the full impact of evil – coming from a cupboard in the kitchen.

'It was strong, very strong indeed, and it hit me as I pulled open the door. I felt something grab me by the neck and it was as if teeth were biting into me. There was nothing there, nothing that could be seen, but I was being choked by something. I couldn't breathe and my limbs seemed to be paralysed.'

His colleagues grabbed his arms to support him and began praying loudly and fervently. 'And as they prayed the hold on me seemed to relax,' he said. 'The demon was still attacking me, because it saw me as its immediate adversary, but it was getting weaker . . . and I was able to give the command of banishment.'

Suddenly the air seemed 'cleaner and warmer'.

'I knew then that the place had been delivered from evil. I don't know how long it had been in the house, or what had attracted it in the first place, but I am convinced that it had caused the death of that young man. And, if my friends hadn't been there, it might well have killed me.'

Evil spirits, according to many exorcists, occasionally continue fighting long after being evicted. 'There have been several cases of cast-out demons dogging exorcists for days,' said Mr Gemmell. 'They want revenge. They also want to batter their way into the exorcists and stay there in control.' That sounded a rather fanciful and extravagant statement, but it was subsequently endorsed by other exorcists, including men regarded as experts within the Church of England, such as the Revd J. Dover-Wellman of Hampstead, in London.

Father Clare is among the priests who claim to have suffered one of these 'aftermath attacks'. He describes it as the most nightmarish experience in his long career as an exorcist. And it happened because he made a mistake. He misjudged the strength and deviousness of a demon.

Most people would have been mentally and emotionally scarred by the ordeal which Father Clare describes having undergone soon after getting a telephone call at his home in Devon. He was saved by his great faith but he was severely jolted and frightened.

The call was from the father of a seventeen-year-old, Malcolm Hill*, whose personality had changed dramatically after he had taken LSD. He had gone on three mind-expanding trips, unknown to his parents, and it was the third which resulted in havoc. He veered between periods of total apathy and brief bouts of unprovoked violence. When he switched into one of his unpredictable savage moods, he would screech and become physically violent. He was like a tornado of a boy. Then, in an instant, the fit would be over. He would again be silent and listless – giving the impression that he could no longer see or hear, that he was oblivious to other people and to his surroundings.

They took Malcolm to doctors and psychiatrists and he was given medication to subdue the violence. But his rages continued to flare occasionally, erupting through the mild sedatives, and then he was difficult to restrain. He had to leave his public school and a psychiatrist recommended that he should be admitted to a mental hospital. This was not with a view to curing him in the foreseeable future but because he was considered too dangerous to stay at home. It was then, as a last resort, that Mr Hill sought the help of Father Clare.

Does LSD make a person more vulnerable to possession? There is a conflict of opinion between experts. Many ridicule the concept of such a link because they regard 'possession' as superstitious nonsense. Others readily accept the possibility but disagree about the likely reason. One commonly accepted theory is based on the premise that each of us is surrounded by a psychic aura, a form of invisible armour, which serves as a protection. LSD is then believed to do temporary or even permanent damage to that armour – so making it easier for an individual to be invaded by 'psychic parasites'. Others argue that the drug exposes a user to this side-effect danger by tilting the mind off-balance and undermining its health. They hold that an unhealthy mind, like an unhealthy body, is more susceptible to attack – with the attacker, in this case, more likely to be a spiritual entity than a virus.

Some people can go on hallucinogenic trips repeatedly without any apparent psychic backlash. Malcolm Hill, Father Clare suspected, was less fortunate. The behaviour pattern described by Mr Hill, coupled with the psychiatrists' failure to agree on a diagnosis, made him feel there was a possibility that Malcolm was being controlled by an alien spirit.

* * *
* * *

Father Clare examined Malcolm carefully, not so much with his eyes as with the power of his clairvoyant concentration, and he claims to have identified damage to Malcolm's aura. There was also, he felt, an atmosphere of evil – similar to that described by other priests – and this convinced him that the boy was demon-possessed. Malcolm remained docile and detached, apparently disinterested.

Father Clare explained the situation to the parents. The entity was rather like a limpet clinging to their son – squeezing its influence into him and constantly replenishing its own energy by sucking it in from the atmosphere around.

The concept is easier to grasp if one thinks of it as a noxious weed in a bed of delicate flowers. The head, leaves and stem can be clearly seen but it flourishes because of the nourishment from its hidden roots. This invisible transmission of power into the entity would have to be stopped. The entity would not then die as a weed would die – for the cutting-off could be only a short-term measure – but it would be prevented from drawing immediately on the great reservoir of evil. The amount of energy available to it would be restricted during the crucial time of exorcism.

How could this be achieved?

Father Clare uses salt. 'Casting a circle of salt around an undesirable entity is similar to snipping a telephone line,' he says. 'The line can be restored when the affected person leaves the circle, with communications flowing again, but by then the entity should have been expelled . . .'

Plato described salt as 'a substance dear to the gods' and Homer called it 'divine' but why should it be considered valuable in twentieth-century exorcisms? Does this not savour of irrational superstition?

Salt is a traditional cleansing element and many exorcists believe it also cleanses on a spiritual level. Father Clare says, 'It is most difficult to explain to those who have no conception of the vast ramifications of the life forces which surround us but salt can neutralise any vibrations or energy frequencies which are out of harmony. It sterilises evil.'

He and Malcolm stood in the centre of the room while he sprinkled raw salt around them on the carpet. Father Clare is a white-haired and powerfully-built man who, even in casual conversation, has an air of calm authority. Now he was facing the boy, close to him inside the circle of salt, and his expression was commandingly stern. Malcolm was still virtually in a trance. His eyes were uncomprehendingly dull as Father Clare sprinkled him with holy water. Father Clare's voice became louder and more compellingly firm: 'By the virtue of the power vested in me . . . in the Name which above every name, in the power of the Father . . .' Slowly, with great deliberation, he made the sign of the Cross. '. . . and of the Son . . .' His fingers traced another Cross. '. . . and of the Holy Ghost . . .' He was watching Malcolm intently as he outlined the Cross for the third time. 'I exorcise this influence of evil . . .' As he uttered these words he splashed more holy water on Malcolm – at the top of his head and at the front of his throat, at the nape of his neck and by his heart.

Malcolm's aura seemed to have cleared almost immediately and even Father Clare was surprised.

He had expected the 'possessing demon' to fight and had been prepared to combat it, if necessary, with further prayers and commands. And with what he regards as additional potent aids – such as the incense of juniper berries and laurel leaves burning on charcoal.

Juniper also has medical antiseptic properties, considered to be effective against sicknesses such as yellow fever, and is regarded by many exorcists as another powerful cleanser of 'polluted atmospheres'. The same is true of laurel which, although a narcotic which in excess can cause death, was used to treat venereal disease.

Father Clare says he would certainly have used them in incense form – if he had not made the mistake of underestimating his adversary.

Malcolm blinked repeatedly, looked around the room in surprise as if seeing it for the first time. 'What's happening here?' he asked. 'What's going on?'

He was bright and lucid but had no recollection of the journey or of entering the house. Long after dark that night, when he was alone in the house, Father Clare was awakened by a terrible clattering from the kitchen downstairs. He went to investigate and the noises stopped as he neared the kitchen. Nothing in the room seemed to have been disturbed. There was no sign of any creature.

There was no further disturbance but the following night brought an alarming repetition. At about two o'clock he heard thuds coming from his study across the landing, and it sounded as if furniture was being hurled around. 'I got out of bed and stood there listening and I realised then exactly what was happening,' he said. 'The evil entity which had come out of the boy was still in my house. It was virtually challenging me to a duel because it wanted to possess me and take over my priestly powers. What a prize I, a priest, would be! There was no alternative but to meet it head on. Only then could I fight it effectively.'

He hurried downstairs to prepare for battle. In the kitchen he added juniper berries and laurel leaves to his charcoal censer which, to speed the process, he heated on an electric ring. Then, armed with the censer and a cannister of raw salt, he went to the door of his study. He paused briefly on the landing, saying a silent prayer, before flinging the door open. Immediately he was aware of a strangely acrid smell which he associates with evil.

The metal-framed chair by his desk had been toppled. Books and papers had been scattered from the desk and the floor was strewn with the contents of drawers and cupboards. Yet there was no sound in the study now and no hint of movement.

He stepped into the room, scattering salt in wide arcs, and shouted a command: 'Come forth!'

Father Clare has devoted many years to studying the psychic world and is convinced that discarnate spirits, manipulating elemental forces, can appear in the guise of flesh-and-blood realities. He regards this as an explanation for many sightings of 'ghosts'. Reassuring apparitions of newly-dead loved ones often materialise in this way. So do grotesque spectres spawned by hatred or depravity. He was anticipating the possibility of suddenly seeing his enemy – in one form or another – but, even so, he was not fully prepared for the imminent appalling confrontation . . .

He was near the centre of the room now, standing on the salt, and once again he rasped out the order: 'Come forth!'

Immediately he had the impression of evil energy swirling around him, growing rapidly in strength as though surging towards some monumental climax. And in a corner he saw the phantom shape created by his adversary. It was basically that of a gigantic man with talons on its webbed paws and with the head of a long-haired ape.

Far-fetched? I would have been tempted to dismiss this account as absurd if other exorcists, including the Revd J. Dover-Wellman, a veteran priest in the Church of England, had not testified to having had comparable experiences. I have questioned these men closely and their accounts strike me as too detailed, too matchingly confirmative, to be lightly discounted.

Father Clare describes how, in a startled reflex, he flung his censer straight at the apparition. 'There was a huge flare of light and, in that instant, the apparition went. The devil had created that monstrous sight, which certainly looked solid, in a bid to capture me. Terror changes people, makes them vulnerable. They are not fully in possession of themselves when in a state of acute fear. They have chinks in their psychic armour, like those which made the boy so vulnerable, and those chinks are open doorways for evil. This particular force of evil knew that its potent weapon against me was fear.'

There he was alone in the shambles of his study, with the remains of herbs and charcoal smouldering on the floor. He stamped on them. The room was pungent with incense but he could no longer feel the presence of evil. He went right through the house to satisfy himself that it was now entirely 'clean'. Then he prayed for the blessing of God.

Father Clare has no obvious motive for embellishment. He is a private man who does not court publicity. He is also cautious about attributing events, sights or symptoms to any supernatural power: 'Most people who fear they are possessed, or who have been told they are possessed, are not so at all. The majority have some form of mental problem which is properly a matter for the psychiatrists. Some of the others are obsessed with themselves or are simply yearning for notoriety. Only in a small minority of cases is there a genuine penetration by evil. In those cases the only solution is exorcism.'

Why should it be possible for certain exorcists to have such vivid visions of evil while others, who claim to have experienced its physical attacks, have never actually *seen* it? A pointer could lie in the fact that some have less psychic awareness and so feel the need to work in partnership with clairvoyants.

A short-sighted man may refuse to accept that there are sheep on a distant hill – simply because he can see no sheep. If his vision were better, very likely he would see them and acknowledge their existence. Is it not just possible that most of us have a comparable partial blindness concerning entities in the psychic realm? Should we not be prepared to concede that they may be there, visible to people with powerful 'second sight', although they are not visible through our eyes?

This could explain why descriptions of spirit sightings, which may sound totally unbelievable, are often given by those claiming to have psychic gifts.

Eric Myers is a lay exorcist and healer who uses such gifts. His interest in the psychic world was initially stimulated when, as an army captain, he was engaged in intelligence work in West Africa. One of his native drivers was a *ju-ju* man and, through him, Mr Myers was introduced to other practitioners of magic.

Later he was posted to Egypt where he studied the occult mysteries of the Middle East. He is a briskly practical man who, whilst recognising the power of spirits, always suspected accounts of attempted assaults by phantasmagoria.

His opinion changed dramatically at the home of friends in Buckinghamshire when he came face to face with an enraged devil.

The twenty-six-year-old daughter of the house had problems which had become apparent, like those of Malcolm Hill, shortly after she had started experimenting with drugs. She had been a cheerfully extrovert woman, particularly fond of swimming and riding, and had a promising career with a bank. But she became addicted to drugs and eventually to alcohol. She was starting to deteriorate, mentally and physically.

She resigned from her job and stayed home. Her mother attempted to curb the drinking and drug-taking. The family doctor arranged for her to see a psychiatrist and eventually she was weaned off the addictions. Yet there seemed to be no improvement in her physical or mental health – with bouts of severe depression coming more frequently – and, as the months went by, this puzzled the psychiatrist.

She told her parents that only one fear was preventing her suicide: the act would involve abandoning her pet dog for which, despite her problems, she had great affection. Her parents, although distressed, did not believe there was real danger. People seriously considering suicide, they felt, did not talk about it for week after week.

Suddenly the dog became mysteriously and violently ill. A veterinary surgeon saved its life and then their daughter admitted that she had given it poison – so that it 'would not be left to grieve' after her death.

About a month later Mollie and Eric Myers arrived for a weekend break. He told me: 'The daughter seemed comparatively normal when we got there, apart from being rather more reserved than in the past, and she certainly didn't strike me as looking ill. Her parents had told me about her behaviour and I believed she probably had some mental problem which might be alleviated by the laying-on of hands.'

It did not occur to him, he says, that the woman might be harbouring a demon.

Many healers describe experiencing warmth in their hands when a laying-on session is being effective and Mr Myers says he had the feeling that day. He was confident that the woman was being helped – not by him but through him – and he decided they should have another session that evening. Later, with hindsight, he believed that the initial session disturbed and provoked an evil entity inside the woman – that the entity, in a self-defence bid to drive him away, created a form of nightmare.

He says that the afflicted woman was walking across the room towards him, as they were about to have a meal, when he saw her features change. Others seated at the table, including his wife, saw nothing unusual but he claims to have glimpsed the controlling spirit of evil.

He said: 'Just for a few seconds she was transformed from a fairly ordinary young lady into a hideous and wizened old crone. She was hunched and scrawny and her face was all sunken and she looked at least ninety years old. Her eyes were glowing with hatred and I was aware of a putrid stench, like that of rotting vegetation. Then the smell went as quickly as it had come and the girl looked just as she'd done when we'd arrived. It was as if the elemental spirit, which I now realised was possessing her, had virtually overflowed for a fraction of time and had completely enveloped her.'

Mr Myers decided to perform an exorcism and prepared to do so immediately in the kitchen. He uses words and ritual movements which are embraced in the cabbala – a mystic science said to have been divinely imparted to the early Hebrews.

His own protection had to be secure before he started, for he felt that, in challenging this power of evil, he could be vulnerable as a target. He prayed silently for the four archangels – Gabriel, Michael, Uriel and Raphael – to surround him as sentinels of strength. Gabriel is regarded as the messenger of divine comfort.

He uttered the prescribed words as he made the sign of the Cross. As he touched his forehead he said '*Ator*' (Thou art). He touched his lower abdomen and said *'Malkuth'* (the Kingdom). He completed the Cross by touching his right and left shoulders with the words *'Ve-Gevurah . . . Ve-Gedulan'* (And the Power . . . and the Glory).

Facing east, he clasped his hands together before his chest and said *'Le-Olahim'* (Forever) followed by 'Amen'. The ancients regarded the sun, which rises in the east, as the Father of Life. That is why this traditional ritual requires the exorcist to face the east. Mr Myers was now ready for battle.

He looked the woman firmly in the eyes and addressed himself to the entity inside her: 'Whoever you are and wherever you are from, leave this person and come forth.' Nothing happened. He repeated the command more forcibly. Still nothing. The exorcism was not being successful.

Occasionally exorcists believe they are facing an entity which is too entrenched for them to evict on their own and they may then seek assistance, returning to the battle later as part of a team. Mr Myers felt that he was tackling such an entity. In retrospect, he knows he was being deceived by the slyness of the spirit; it had left the woman but was lingering around the house.

Later, in the presence of his wife and the mother, he saw the hag again. She was 'hovering outside the kitchen window, a few feet above the ground, with her arms outstretched and her fingers pointing as if in a threat'.

'She looked like a gruesome pantomime witch and her eyes were fixed on me. Suddenly she launched herself straight at me, coming right through the glass of the closed window, and she was making a horrible screeching noise. I prayed in that instant for the protection of the archangels and she was within a couple of feet of me when a golden sword suddenly materialised in front of me. She was impaled on it and immediately she lost all shape and turned into a column of black smoke which dwindled into a whisp and then vanished. I knew then that she was really gone, that she'd been completely destroyed.'

Neither his wife nor their hostess saw or heard this 'phantom witch'. But both saw the astonishing effect that 'something' had on Eric Myers. Mrs Myers told me, 'At one moment he was talking quite normally and then, for no obvious reason, he went white and stiff with fear. He was staring towards the window and muttering something which we couldn't catch and, afterwards, it took him a long time to stop shaking.'

Eric Myers admits that at one time he'd have regarded such a story with scepticism. He had heard accounts of evil becoming manifest in this way but had felt they 'savoured of the old legends about werwolves and churchyard vampires'.

The sudden appearance of the golden sword might be regarded as a rather unlikely display of melodrama on the part of the Almighty. But it could also be seen as logical answer to prayer. In that moment of terror, Mr Myers needed instant reassurance. He needed tangible evidence of God's protection – in a form he could recognise immediately.

Many religious leaders refuse to believe that spiritual forces, whether baleful or benevolent, can assume any visible shape. There is mounting evidence to suggest that these men could be making an enormous mistake.

2 Confronting black magic

Are there people who have the power to summon evil spirits and to direct them into acts of grotesque violence? Such power is commonly accepted as an indisputable reality in many primitive parts of the world. The possibility is also being taken very seriously in civilised countries which, during the past ten years, have witnessed an accelerating interest in the occult. By 1981 experts in the Christian churches, including the veteran Benedictine exorcist Dom Robert Petitpierre, were estimating that at least 40,000 self-proclaimed witches or magicians were practising in Britain. But the true figure is undoubtedly greater because most of the ceremonies are conducted in secrecy in unexpected venues such as council houses or small bungalows in sedate suburbia. Many of the 'practitioners in the black arts' are pathetic and self-deluding inadequates, mentally or emotionally unbalanced, who have become morbidly obsessed by the unknown. There are others, however, who unquestionably can wreak havoc – even if only because their claims are believed, and feared, by their potential victims.

An increasing number of these victims, convinced they have become possessed because of a curse, now seek the help of exorcists.

I met one of them at St Saviour's Church, Hampstead, on a drab, overcast morning in April. She was a Kenyan in her early twenties who had been brought up in Britain, a quietly self-composed and ordinary-looking woman. She was sharp witted and articulate. But she began to change, speaking hesitantly and almost apologetically – her eyes apprehensive as if she was anticipating disbelief – when she started to describe an ordeal which had been obscenely horrendous.

She claimed that she had been raped repeatedly by a violent force of evil. These assaults had been occurring week after week, for more than seven months. Although her assailant had no flesh or blood, no shape which could be seen, it was so tangibly real that she could feel it surge through sexual climaxes.

We were in the vestry of the church where the vicar, the Reverend Christopher Neil-Smith, would soon be striving to end the torment which had started soon after the woman had left her husband. Their marriage had been a battleground for years. Her husband was frequently in a drunken rage and the previous summer she had taken their young daughter to live with her mother. She was convinced that her husband had decided she should be punished for this desertion, that he had paid for the punishment to be inflicted by an African witch.

She described the demoniac rape: 'For about a week I'd felt as if there was some terrible weight pressing in on me from my waist right down to my toes. My chest, arms and head were free but it was as if there was a tight elastic garment on the lower half of my body. I couldn't get rid of it and I saw the doctor twice because I thought I had some disease. He couldn't find anything wrong.

'One night the pressure eased around my waist and hips. Then nearly all the force, the energy or whatever, that had been clamping in on me seemed to be concentrated between my legs. I was in bed at the time and I couldn't control my legs any more. It was as if there were hands down there, forcing them apart.

'I screamed and tried to push my legs together but I wasn't strong enough. There was no one else in the room but then I could feel this thing pushing into me. The bed began to shake and the springs made noises. I was wide awake and I wasn't imagining it. I really was being raped. Then, afterwards, the pressure was back around my waist.'

So was this some neurotic fantasy or perhaps an indication of erotic wish-fulfilment? Had she been indulging in half-asleep masturbation with images of stimulation that had grown into a non-existent reality?

The concept of physical rape by an entity from a different

dimension – one being controlled rather like a puppet by some backstreet witch – does put a strain on credulity. Yet many who might be inclined to dismiss her account as preposterous may well believe that physical contact – sometimes severe enough to be painful or even dangerous – can be made by alien entities.

Vast numbers of violent manifestations have been reported – with people claiming to have been attacked physically by forces of evil – and much of the evidence is accepted, by those competent to judge, as being well within the bounds of possibility.

The experience described by this young woman introduces an additional and more fundamentally disturbing ingredient because we have here a grotesque perversion of sexuality. Rape of any kind is a singularly degrading crime which provokes angry disgust and, in these extraordinary circumstances, a natural and understandable revulsion could make some people instantly put up a protective barrier of disbelief.

My initial reaction was one of caution. I was prepared to believe that she might be genuinely confused – or an attention-seeking hysteric – but at the same time I did not consider that her story should be dismissed.

She went on to say that her devil rapist occasionally had an accomplice – a large black man with a bald head. 'He would hold my shoulders and press me back against the pillows while the thing raped me. He never said anything and then, when it was over, he would simply disappear.'

There was no black man. That is certain. However, I am not saying she was telling a lie. One must consider the possibility that she was being attacked by a spiritual entity which was using elemental forces to create the illusion of that figure. And, similarly, the 'hands' which held her against the pillows could have been pressure generated by the vibrations of evil.

Initially the woman was unaware that her husband had paid curse-money to a witch. She was told this by a friend who advised her to go to the church for help. A Roman Catholic priest blessed her and the house with holy water. The problems remained. The lower half of her body, she said, was still gripped by that 'elastic garment' and the rapes continued with greater frequency.

Soon there were other horrors – luminous 'devil faces' which would occasionally appear on her wardrobe door and then slowly vanish. Eventually, in desperation, she contacted the Reverend Neil-Smith, who is probably the most famous official exorcist in the Church of England. He is a specialist who has performed more than three thousand casting-out ceremonies – often averaging ten or more a week – and he is recognised as one of the most experienced exorcists in the world.

Many priests claim they can identify vibrations of evil. Mr Neil-Smith regards this ability as an invaluable diagnostic aid as he is keenly aware that mental sickness can be confused with possession. He recognises that the well-intentioned meddlings of over-enthusiastic exorcists can create dangers – sometimes ending in tragedy – and he does not hesitate in referring certain people to psychiatrists. This is a two-way arrangement as patients are often recommended to him by psychiatrists.

In the vestry of his church I could not feel the vibrations of evil which Mr Neil-Smith reported were coming strongly from this frightened and bewildered young woman. Beyond the closed door, below the candle lit altar, her mother and daughter were already kneeling in prayer. They had been advised to be present as an 'antiseptic precaution' because, as a result of living with her, they had been exposed to contamination.

'Ready?'

The woman nodded pensively. He led her into the cavernous old church where she joined her relatives at the altar rail. The unseasonal sombreness of the morning outside was pressing against the inadequate and dusty windows and, beyond the pool of altar light, the distant rear pews were little more than shadows. No-one else was permitted into the church and all doors were locked. Many priests are convinced that a successful exorcism can bring the danger of demonic transference – with a cast-out entity immediately seeking a new human 'lodging' – and that all those present are potentially in jeopardy. Mr Neil-Smith had urged me to seek protection, throughout the ritual, in continual prayer. I was to watch from a near-by choir pew.

Mr Neil-Smith approached the mother. His expression was

sombrely pugnacious as he made the sign of the Cross over her head and then his voice, normally rather quiet, resounded confidently like a challenge through the church: 'I bind by the true God, the living God, the Holy God, all forces of evil, sorcery and black magic that they may not interfere with, disturb or distort your soul.'

The afflicted woman, still kneeling, had her eyes closed. Her head was bowed and her hands were together in prayer.

Now the exorcist was cleaving at the air over her mother's head as if wielding a heavy broadsword: 'I cut with the Sword of the Holy Spirit all psychic links between . . .'

Here he named her daughter and son-in-law before stepping closer to her and clasping her head firmly with both hands: 'O God, Son of God, Unconquered Might . . . beat down Satan under our feet and cause this witchcraft to depart and give place to Christ . . .'

He held the woman briefly, silently offering more prayers. He then repeated the ceremony with the child but she, like her grandmother, did not react. And it was the same, at first, when he was exorcising the afflicted woman. The tracing of the Cross over her lowered head brought no obvious response and neither did the slashing with the symbolic sword. She seemed to be serenely detached, virtually unaware of his presence, and totally immersed in private devotions. But the atmosphere began to change, suddenly and dramatically, when he put his hands on her head. She started to quiver.

He began the supplication: 'Beat down Satan under our feet and cause this witchcraft to depart . . .'

Those words appeared to galvanise her, or whatever it was that was possessing her, into acute anxiety. Now there was no serenity. There was a turmoil of dread. She moaned and convulsed backwards, as though trying to jerk herself further from the altar, but his powerful fingers, entwined in her hair, pressed her back close to him.

'No!' she shouted. 'No . . . no . . . no . . . no!'

Priests in the Roman Catholic Church are given clear instructions about how to proceed when they meet this type of reaction. These instructions are contained in General Rules for

Exorcism, authorised by the Vatican, which stipulate that an exorcist 'will pay attention as to what words in particular cause the evil spirits to tremble, repeating them the more frequently'. They continue: 'If he perceives that he is making progress, let him persist . . . until victory is attained.'

Most exorcists, whatever their faith, adopt this pattern. Mr Neil-Smith started doing so now.

'Cause this witchcraft to depart . . .' he repeated.

'No! *No!*'

Veins were bulging in his neck and his face was flushed with the effort of wrestling to restrain the woman. She was shuddering and writhing, as if in terror, and making low choking noises. The church was chill, smelling slightly of dankness, but he was sweating heavily as he kept repeating the key words, quickly and urgently now, in a low and near-hypnotic monotone.

'Cause this witchcraft to depart and give place to Christ!'

The child was staring fixedly at the altar, hearing the struggle and the sounds of distress from her mother but not daring to turn her head, and the grandmother was leaning forward over the rail to watch in anxious wonderment.

Suddenly the woman's body slumped, as if drained of strength, and Mr Neil-Smith immediately jerked her arms out to form a cross. She was still and tranquil. It was over. He put his hands back on her head, gently now as in a caress, and for a few moments he stood there in silent prayer.

I joined them at the rail, kneeling as he had suggested, and he annointed each of our foreheads with the Cross in holy water.

Many of Mr Neil-Smith's exorcisms are so violent that he gives the impression of literally trying to shake devils out on to the floor of the church. 'It may look as if I'm struggling with the person but that's not it at all. What's really happening is that the evil force is receiving – and fighting to resist – the power of God flowing through my hands. I can feel it with tinglings and sharp stinging sensations in my palms and fingers . . .'

When I later spoke to the woman she could remember little of what had happened at the peak of the exorcism. She had no recollection of shouting out or of trying to jerk away from the altar rail. 'But I feel cleaner and that terrible tightness I had around me . . . it's just gone.'

The fact that she was unaware initially of any attempted curse may seem to indicate that she had been possessed, that she had been tormented by a controlled force of evil. However, it is not necessarily that simple. She knew her husband would be immensely angry over her 'desertion' and that, in view of his nature, he would want her to be punished. She also knew that he had contacts who could probably help him find a 'specialist in the occult'. So one might reasonably wonder if her problems had not developed out of her dread. Anxiety and fear can distort a person's thinking. In an excitable person, particularly, fixations and fantasies can form during a prolonged period of stress or mental morbidity – and they can flourish, becoming progressively stronger, unless firmly eradicated. It is conceivable that her faith in the exorcism, in the compassionate power of God, had rid her of dread rather than of any devil.

Mr Neil-Smith states categorically: 'She was possessed by a very powerful force of evil. It was cast out of her – not by me, of course, but by God.'

I monitored her progress over the next few months and she maintained there had been no more rapes, no further sign of the phantom black man, no suggestion of any lingering evil. She was fit and happy. So on one issue there can be no dispute; whatever the source of her torment, she did receive great benefit from that service of exorcism.

* * *
* * *

The Reverend David MacInnes of Birmingham Cathedral is the offical adviser on exorcism in the Diocese of Birmingham. He claims that he regularly confronts evil generated by witches or magicians – and that frenzied attempts to get away from a priest are often made by possessed people during successful exorcisms.

In a busy month he performs as many as twenty exorcisms. The main reason for this high number, he says, is that his territory contains 'a number of serious occult groups including ones practising satanism'.

One of those he has exorcised was a woman in her twenties, a devout Baptist, who was 'invaded' while trying to draw a young girl away from witchcraft.

Mr MacInnes told me about the girl: 'She'd had a particularly unhappy upbringing, mostly in children's homes, and she was emotionally deprived. This made her vulnerable to feelers put out by the witchcraft group for she saw in that group a form of companionship. She felt that in them she'd found a niche where she could really belong. It was a group which tried to arouse evil through acts of sacrilege such as tearing Bibles, as well as through ceremonies of animal sacrifice and sexual intercourse on an altar.'

The Baptist had met the girl, felt pity for her, and had tried to rescue her. This attempt led to a meeting with the leaders of the group.

'She didn't realise the dangers she was stepping into – or the insidious power of these people. She was persuaded to have intercourse with one of the men and she left a broken woman. Her personality changed after that night and soon she became deeply addicted to drugs.'

She was taken to a rehabilitation centre where she was seen by Mr MacInnes. For a year he prayed regularly for her recovery but it was not until she had made a full confession of what had happened, giving details which she had been too ashamed to mention earlier, that he decided to perform an exorcism.

'As I commanded the evil to leave her she showed clear physical and verbal reactions. She turned away from me, cringing and holding her head in her hands, and she kept repeating "No . . . No. You must not do it . . ." '

He claims that the woman's sanity was restored by the exorcism and that she is now active again as a Christian.

* * *

* * *

Many of those who cast dangerously potent curses – or who claim to do so – insist that their power is not weakened by distance. They are controlling spiritual entities which can travel at the speed of thought and intended victims many thousands of miles away can be made to suffer instantly. Exorcists have similar confidence in their ability to counter evil at long range and in the instantaneous world-spanning power of prayer.

Father Ian Hazlewood had a relative living in Australia who unwittingly incurred the wrath of an aboriginal magic-man – a specialist in aiming curses by pointing bones. This particular curse was designed to cause blindness rather than death.

Severe pain was experienced by the victim but the early symptoms indicated an easily explainable medical cause. The man had been fifty miles out in the bush, visiting friends near the home of the magic man, when his left eye became acutely inflamed. It began to swell and protrude and he thought he'd been bitten by an insect. That was what doctors also believed but they were puzzled when the eye did not respond to treatment. Its condition continued to deteriorate.

Father Hazlewood told me: 'My relative told me on the telephone that the doctors were completely bemused.' The prognosis was that the sight would be permanently lost in the eye.

Then, through his friends in the bush, the man learned about the curse. He repeated this to Father Hazlewood who says he had already performed many successful 'absent-healing' exorcisms. Father Hazlewood explained: 'In those cases, for which I don't need permission from my Bishop, I either take a photograph of the person to the church or I concentrate on forming a picture of them in my mind. On this occasion I didn't need a photograph.'

At his vicarage in Gloucestershire, determined to help a man on the other side of the world, he prepared himself by reciting the Protection Prayer known as Saint Patrick's Breastplate:

Christ be with me
Christ within me
Christ behind me
Christ before me

Christ beside me
Christ to win me
Christ to comfort and restore me
Christ beneath me
Christ above me
Christ in quiet and
Christ in danger
Christ in hearts of all that love me
Christ in mouth of friend and stranger.

Then he went alone to the church where he focussed his thoughts on his relative and on the evil he believed to be inside his relative:

'I command this primitive to depart from [he named the man] and, harming no-one, to return to the place prepared for it. In the name of the Father and of the Son and of the Holy Spirit.' During this command he made the sign of the Cross three times.

That was all. A short and simple ceremony. And the outcome? 'My relative recovered rapidly and completely,' said Father Hazlewood. 'Later, taking time differences into consideration, we established that the improvement started while I was still in the church.'

It might be held that this was nothing more than a coincidence and that a diagnostic error had been made by the medical team. A recovery of this nature, in isolation, could easily be rationalised. My researches have shown, however, that it should not be considered in isolation. Other priests have given evidence of a similar nature and so have medical experts. Here is a pattern which merits serious consideration by those – inside and outside the churches – who flatly reject the idea that there could be any value in exorcism.

* * *
* * *

Evil can be 'bounced back' for miles at its human manipulators, according to the Reverend Neil-Smith, if countered effectively with the power of prayer. They can then experience the backlash of terror.

He was awakened in the early hours by the telephone. A distraught man on the line was begging for help: 'I'm dying . . . right now, this very moment. I'm being killed by voodoo . . .'

The story was disjointed and at times completely incoherent – with the man lapsing into what seemed like hysterical gibberish – but Mr Neil-Smith, repeating questions patiently, gradually pieced it together.

It seemed that the caller had once belonged to a group practising witchcraft. Other members had been angered when he returned to Christianity – and one of them, he was now claiming, was attacking him with a form of voodoo.

'I told him firmly that he was not dying but he was getting more and more desperate,' said Mr Neil-Smith. 'He seemed to be having difficulty breathing, as if he was being slowly choked, and for twenty minutes I prayed with him on the telephone. I prayed for the evil to be pulled out of him and sent away . . .'

The man seemed calmer and his breathing was once again normal. 'But this was merely an emergency, middle of the night solution and I felt it could be only a temporary one,' said Mr Neil-Smith. 'I told him to come to the church, immediately after breakfast, for a full exorcism.'

When the man arrived Mr Neil-Smith knew instantly from the vibrations that he was tackling a 'truly murderous force'. The exorcism was a success but the matter was far from being over.

'Within about an hour I had a stranger at the door, absolutely shaking with fear. This was the man who had cast the spell. He confessed that he'd cast similar ones often before but on this occasion, for the first time, it had gone horrifyingly wrong. He'd apparently had the most awful sensation of being near to death at precisely the time I'd been praying on the telephone with his victim. He'd suddenly felt as if he was suffocating, as if he was suffering the ordeal which he'd created for the other man. He'd been so frightened and bemused that he'd called at the man's home, just after the man had left for the church, to find what sort of counter-magic had been invoked.

'There'd been a strong spiritual link between the three of us at that particular time because the voodoo man and I had both been concentrating on the victim. My prayers had pulled much of the evil out of the man and that evil had then gone back along the link like a boomerang. It had come close to destroying the man who had generated it and he was terrified that it might still do so. He felt he now needed the help of God.

'I took him into the church where he renounced the devil and all his works. He also made a solemn oath that he would never again dabble in voodoo or witchcraft. Then we went to his home to collect all his black-magic books and manuscripts and we burned them in a corner of the churchyard.'

Can we believe that this man was attacked by a self-invoked force of evil because of prayers by a priest? Does the concept of such an attack not seem a contradiction of the loving gentleness preached by Christians?

'As we forgive those who trespass against us . . .' That line in the Lord's Prayer is hardly a request for adversaries to be punished. So is it logical to accept that supplications to God could really cause such terror and distress? It might be felt that, in a situation of this nature, the answer should be 'yes'.

'Deliver us from evil . . .' Many people utter that plea regularly without giving it deep thought, without pausing to consider the possible mechanics of such deliverance.

Now let us consider the circumstances in this particular case. The 'voodoo man' was working on his victim telepathically at the time, concentrating hard on his destruction, and it could be argued that this effort had to be neutralised. His temporary disabilitating torment could then be seen as an essential part of the answer to prayer.

3 Manipulators of evil?

Ceremonies of exorcism are performed frequently by self-proclaimed witches and magicians. Many of these men and women claim that they have a far deeper understanding of spiritual evil than most priests – being closer to it and having spent years experimenting with it – and that their ability to combat it is therefore stronger.

They often invoke the protection of ancient gods which were worshipped long before the birth of Christ. And their 'safeguards' occasionally involve nauseating rituals, such as one described by Captain Barry Irons of the Church Army – the evangelical arm of the Church of England – who is a specialist in exorcism: 'Two cats are pinned together with a wooden stake in the shape of a cross, while they are still alive. Their stomachs are ripped open and the blood is collected in a vessel – sometimes a human skull taken from a graveyard – from which each member of the group takes a sip. The cats are still alive at this stage and set alight. They die in terrible agony.'

It is tempting to feel that these people are nothing more than sadistic lunatics. Should we take any of them seriously?

There are many experts in the churches, including the Liverpool exorcist Father Robert Brunswick, who insist it would be foolhardy not to do so. They endorse a warning given to me by Father Hazlewood: 'Don't underestimate the potency of black magic. It can be very strong indeed and we, as Christians, would be failing in our duty if we did not recognise that fact. Of course, there are a great number of deluded people who imagine, quite wrongly, that they can command occult forces. But there are also those who genuinely have the power to attract and manipulate evil, who can use it to invoke curses and to attack other people.'

David Marriott claims to have such power. He has used it to launch spiritual assaults on enemies and to help friends who have become possessed.

He is an ardent admirer of the late Aleister Crowley – who liked to be known as The Beast – and describes himself as a Grand Master of Magic. His home in Luton is called Black Shadows. A back room serves as his temple in which he claims to have practised an advanced form of necromancy. He also claims to have had repeated success there in the exorcising of demoniacs.

Five cowled and black-robed worshippers were near the altar in his tiny temple, where the darkness was broken only by the flame of a stubby red candle, when there was an unexpected eruption of evil. One of the worshippers collapsed and began to howl like a crazed beast. He started writhing in agony and scratched at the floor tiles as if trying to rip them up with his nails. Before the service he had appeared subdued and vaguely apprehensive, but the others had not realised at that stage that he was already filled with dread.

Now his eyes were protruding and his bodily contortions were becoming more frantic. Within minutes Mr Marriott was kneeling beside him to conduct an exorcism.

In the temple shortly afterwards Mr Marriott described how the victim had ritually invited possession.

Our chairs were inside the nine-feet diameter of the magic circle – white pentacles painted on the black floor. The windows were curtained and shuttered, for daylight is never permitted in this incense-laden room, and the altar was dominated by a trepanned skull which held the candle. The skull was on a pedestal below which, on the altar table, were spread the paraphernalia of sorcery – including the hermatic cross and the chalice, the pentacles and magic wand. Near the front was the ornate sword which is 'necessary to activate the magic circle' and the black-handled dagger used to 'subdue and punish rebellious demons'.

Daggers which have been 'blessed and purified' are often used in magic-circle exorcisms when psychic parasites are believed to be in the human aura rather than inside a person. Exorcists stab at them and the tips of the blades, it is claimed, discharge small but exterminating thunderbolts. Many magicians prefer a sophisticated variant, with a long handle and three sharp prongs, which was used by the German mystic-doctor Paracelsus who died in 1541. It is called the Trident of Paracelsus.

At the back of the table, beside the joss-stick holder and the container for salt, was a twelve-inch doll representing Isis. She was the principal goddess of ancient Egypt and was often depicted as a woman with the horns of a cow. Isis is revered by Mr Marriott and his acolytes, members of the Ancient Order of Oriental Templars, for they believe their power flows largely from her and other deities once worshipped in the region of the Nile. These Egyptian deities, they claim, were protecting the group when the 'possessed man' had his seizure.

Mr Marriott said: 'He'd come to us from another powerful group which had helped him make a pact with a force of evil – a demon which they'd summoned into their temple. He used his own blood to write and sign the pact which promised that the demon could have his soul after ten years. During that time, in return, the man would have the gift of great power in business and with women. I didn't know about this when he joined or I'd have helped him earlier and I'd never allow such a pact to be made here. It is far too dangerous. Using demons for your own benefit, if you have the knowledge and ability, is one thing. Agreeing to give yourself to one is completely different.'

The demon-pact man had been a neophyte at the time of the signing and, according to Mr Marriott, he had been granted 'great power'. 'There was no doubt that, materially, he had been helped enormously for he'd had a tremendous run of success. His life was better than it had ever been but he became apprehensive. He still had nearly two years before he'd have to honour his side of the bargain but, because of his fear, he wanted to break the pact. It seemed that he'd been trying to do so rather clumsily on his own and that was why the demon boiled over with fury.' The entity was deep inside the possessed man, rather than merely infesting his aura, and consequently they could not use the dagger. Others in the group pinned down the man, who was still howling and convulsing violently, while Mr Marriott held his head and kept repeating 'magic words'. He told me: 'I was speaking directly to the demon – commanding it to leave him and the temple and to return to its own sphere. It surrendered after trying to resist for about twenty minutes. The man was then very bewildered for a while, as if he'd been asleep and couldn't grasp what had happened, but after about an hour was back to normal.'

Mr Marriott is a former Methodist who says that, after finding 'other powers as strong as Christ', he graduated through witchcraft to black magic. For years he devoted himself to black magic but, shortly before our meeting, he turned away from it in fear. He claims that he witnessed another black magician destroy the mind of a male victim – that the demonstration so jolted him that he resolved to confine himself in future to white magic which, its practitioners say, is good and beneficial.

He also claims to have invoked curses. He describes making a man seriously ill by writing his name on a triangle of wood and casting a spell of sickness – the type of spell reputed to be strengthened by the blood of a cockerel or a pigeon. He said, 'This man belonged to a group which was in conflict with us. He became my enemy only because there was a power of evil controlling him and, although I didn't really want to harm him, I had to work through him in order to destroy that power.'

There are customers willing to pay for 'tailor-made curses'. Many of the purveyors still favour methods which have been used for centuries. There are those who claim they can create heart troubles by hammering nails into the hearts of sheep. And I know of one who insists she can help the wives of adulterous husbands by driving spikes into the testicles of a ram.

* * *

* * *

Some curses are designed to bring victims into disrepute by affecting their behaviour, by making them commit uncharacteristic acts of crime.

This was exposed at the Old Bailey when a young mechanic denied responsibility for the attempted rape of a student. He told the jury that enemies had put a curse on him: 'For four years I was possessed by a spirit which made me do things I could not control nor understand. I had no intention of hurting or raping her. I was possessed by a force which took over my body and did this dreadful thing.'

This explanation was amplified by defending counsel, Mr Laurence Giovene: 'He was possessed by an exterior force, the devil, which is capable of overpowering the human mind and taking over for a period. He was not in control of his actions when he committed this offence. Jesus Christ was himself an exorcist. There are people today who can also do this and can identify a possessed person. Excorcism is accepted as a reality by the Church of England and the Roman Catholic Church.'

This argument did not impress Judge Neil McKinnon: 'When I was a child we were taught that everything we did wrong was because of Satan and I was walloped even harder.' He asked Mr Giovene: 'Can you point to any authority in the law which indicates that a man can contest a criminal charge by saying he was under the influence of an evil spirit? I am not going to have the time of this court wasted. What is your authority?'

Mr Giovene replied that he considered he had legal authority. He also claimed that some of the judge's comments on the nature of the defence – such as 'I suppose we have got to suffer it' – had placed him in an embarrassing position.

The judge replied: 'You need not be embarrassed. Do you want me to discharge the jury?'

'I think so.'

'Very well. You can have the case tried before a different judge.'

At the Old Bailey three weeks later Judge Edward Clarke let the mechanic go free by imposing a suspended sentence. One can only speculate about the judge's reason for such leniency. The jury had found the man guilty of an extremely serious crime. The sentence would seem to indicate that Judge Clarke felt the defence explanation deserved sympathetic consideration.

The man was exorcised by Mr Neil-Smith who said to me, 'It would have been a travesty to have sent him to prison because, like the girl who was attacked, he was unquestionably a victim. Unfortunately, far too many people still don't realise the tremendous power wielded by followers of the devil.'

* * *
* * *

Christian exorcists often work behind locked doors – to avoid putting unintentional intruders at risk – but have no inhibitions about discussing the details of their ceremonies. Most are eager to help spread a deeper understanding of the ways in which they operate.

This is not the case with those who claim to cast out evil with the aid of non-Christian magic. David Marriott refuses to disclose the 'magic words' used during that exorcism in the Black Shadows temple: 'That knowledge is forbidden to all those who have not taken the First Degree Oath of Secrecy. The penalty for breaking the oath is death.'

That was a convenient reply, some may feel, to cover the nothingness of magic. But his anxiety, as I pressed him harder, was certainly not feigned. Many people claim to have been persecuted telepathically because they have broken oaths of allegiance of this nature. Some have died in strange circumstances.

Many youngsters are ensnared by occult groups, through curiosity. They are apprehensive about the unknown but, at the same time, drawn by its fascination. That is why I feel it may be helpful to strip away some of the mystery, to give an insight into the style of ceremonial, in the hope that it will then lose some of its attraction.

The First Degree Oath of Secrecy involves a rigid pattern of words and actions. After preliminary vetting to establish suitability, a candidate for membership of one of the order's lodges is blindfolded and taken by two officers, the Emir and the Vizier, into the temple which is decorated to represent an oasis. In Moslem countries an Emir is a chieftain and a Vizier a high official.

The candidate is held outside the magic circle while the Emir asks: 'I demand of you – are you free [of any other order] and of full age?'

Satisfactory answers lead to the next question: 'Do you understand that by entering this camp you have incurred the penalty of death?'

'I do.'

The Vizier presses a dagger against the candidate's throat: 'Do you consider the honour of enrolling yourself among us as full compensation for this doom?'

'I do.'

The Vizier responds: 'Advance if free man without fear.'

The initiate is then taken into the circle and the Emir is questioned by the awaiting Grand Master who, during this ceremony, is referred to as Saladin: 'Who have you there?'

'A poor stranger who seeks admission into our camp to learn our mysteries.'

'Is he well vouched for?'

'He is.' The Emir seizes one of the initiate's wrists, applies a dagger to it, and asks: 'Are you prepared to obey and uphold our laws and regulations?'

'I am.'

'And to conform to all our customs and ceremonies?'

'I am.'

'And to persevere through the ceremony of lustration?'

'I am.'

This is the moment for the initiate to be questioned directly by the Grand Master: 'In all cases of difficulty or danger, in whom do you put your trust?'

The initiate will already have been primed with the only acceptable answer: 'Myself.' This follows the precept set out in *The Book of the Law* by Aleister Crowley in which is written: 'Do What Thou Wilt shall be the whole of the Law.'

The initiate then gives this undertaking: 'If I betray the bread and salt and betray the officers and magicians in whose presence I now stand and break my solemn magical oath's obligations, may the gods devour my carcass, may I be mutilated and no longer be a man.'

The use of dagger in this ceremony is purely symbolic. Retribution for a broken oath hardly ever involves an obvious physical attack. Attempts are made to invoke it through ritual curses with members concentrating their mental energies into a 'cone of power' which, when fully-formed, is directed at the victim.

The phrase 'cone of power' may savour of hyperbole but the practice merely mirrors one followed by dedicated Christians. Churches have healing-prayer groups, often meeting in private homes, in which members concentrate collectively on named individuals who are sick or are in some special need of help. These groups are trying through their words, thoughts and rituals, to create 'cones of power'. If it is possible for them to succeed – and vast numbers of Christians are convinced they often do – it would be fatuous to simply dismiss the success claims of magicians.

The final undertaking given by the initiate – 'may I be mutilated and no longer be a man' – envisages the mutilation of his mind, the destruction of himself as a self-possessed individual.

Mr Marriott fears he would be exposed to this type of 'mutilation' if he were to break his First Degree Oath. Long before taking that oath, he had taken another when initiated into a witchcraft coven. He was then taken naked and blindfolded, with the customary dagger at his heart, into the presence of the High Priestess. This is a moment which some witches have described as immensely frightening. Newcomers into this strange realm do not know what to expect and tend to be assailed by last-minute doubts. They feel vulnerable with the blade pressing into their flesh and some can hardly stifle the dread that this might develop into a ceremony of human sacrifice. Such fears are hardly allayed by the standard words: 'If he has fear in his heart it would be better for him to rush upon this blade and perish.'

The newcomer is then annointed with oil and water before being scourged by three senior members of the coven. The whippings sting but do no real physical harm. The High Priestess then kisses the initiate five times, on various parts of the body, and each kiss is accompanied by the greeting 'Blessed be'. A piece of cotton then used to measure the initiate's height is retained by the coven – to be used only if the initiate later tries to break away. It represents the length of ground that he or she would lie in at death.

The oath of allegiance follows and, eventually, the initiate is fully received into the coven through sexual intercourse – often performed symbolically rather than physically by dipping a dagger into a chalice.

Mr Marriott advocates full intercourse: 'Then it is a complete giving of yourself. You are becoming as of one body with the Priestess – or the Priest, in the case of a female – and she represents the entire coven.'

* * *

* * *

Is it possible to talk with the dead? Christians are sharply divided on this question but many insist they do have this ability. Mr Marriott claims that during his black magic years he communicated regularly with the dead and was also able, through secret rites, to recreate the physical body of a long-buried man. He indicated the trepanned skull. 'He died more than a hundred years ago but I brought him back, looking just as he did in life, right here in this temple.' His manner was almost casual, as if this was a mundane statement. 'I summoned his spirit here, as I'd done several times earlier, and directed it into the body of a young woman. She was near the altar at the time, part of my regular group, and she knew little about it because she was in a state of trance.

'The rest of us could see the physical change as her features were transformed and remoulded and suddenly, instead of being a girl, she was a middle-aged man with dark hair and a beard. He was with us in this form, as tangible as anyone else in the temple, for about three minutes. One of the group was so startled that he ran out and was frightened to return.'

Imaginative boasting? A lie designed to impress? Possibly. But I questioned him on a number of occasions about this transformation and his description of the details never varied. Other experts in the occult, including Christian exorcists, consider that his account should certainly not be regarded as impossible.

He added, 'After the three minutes the girl's appearance returned to normal and the spirit hovered over the skull until I performed a ritual of banishment. I had the power to make it come and obey my commands exactly as I wished. And, although I no longer use it, I still have that power.'

* * *

* * *

Even devotees like Mr Marriott warn amateurs against experimenting or becoming involved, unsupervised, with the occult. 'Mental hospitals are littered with people who have done so and who, not appreciating the strength of the forces, have gone right over the edge.'

A similar view is expressed by some psychiatrists. So how many people are exposing themselves to these dangers? How many are being attracted into the 'dark-side' groups? The 1981 estimate of 'at least forty thousand' in Britain was dismissed by Mr Marriott as a 'hopelessly out-of-date figure'.

He said, 'There were more than that in the late 1970s and the numbers have been growing fast. Some of these people, of course, are doing little more than paddling on the edge, but my experience in various groups shows that about five people in a thousand are using power for deep evil.'

So, if he is right, Britain now has more than 200,000 people who are attempting to summon and direct dangerous forces of evil. Perhaps it is not surprising, then, that there is a significant increase in the number of people seeking the help of exorcists.

4 Ouija

One of the most controversial board games ever sold is ouija – derived from the French and German for 'yes' – which was reported in 1981 to have overtaken Monopoly as a best-seller in America. It is designed as a basic tool for novices who want to experiment with spiritualism. The object is to attract spirits of the dead. Priests and self-proclaimed witches are united in the belief that this can be achieved. They are also convinced that ouija can open the door for other forms of spiritual entities – non-human ones which can be balefully dangerous.

The easy availability of ouija-boards was deplored by a witch-coven leader who told me: 'When you've studied it thoroughly and learned from experts, you can keep the spirits under control, but most people have no idea how to deal with the spirits they invoke with these boards. That's when the spirits can take over and cause mayhem.'

One of the most active campaigners against ouija is the Reverend George Tarleton, former Minister of Chingford Congregational Church, who is a leader of the House Church Movement. This is a movement which holds its services in the homes of its congregations, on a rota basis, rather than in churches. Many of its members are radical Christians who have felt disillusioned by what they call 'formal Churchianity'. Mr Tarleton has often appeared on television to attack ouija, which he describes as 'the game in which anyone can play and no one can win'. He claims that physical injuries can be inflicted by 'ouija spirits' and tells of a group of children who decided to test the power which they believed they had attracted: 'They asked it to demonstrate its strength by breaking the leg of one of their friends. This friend was out in the school playground at the time

– not involved with what they were doing – and immediately after their session they found he'd been carted off with a broken ankle. There'd been no one near him and he said later that he'd slipped for no apparent reason . . .'

Mr Tarleton described another instance: 'It was nearly midnight when the phone rang. It was the police. "We've a boy here in the hospital who has been in a trance state for three days. Can you help?"

'The boy was lying on a bed in the ward with his hands crossed and his eyes staring vacantly at the ceiling. I asked where his father was and was told he wouldn't come near his son because he had been so violent. This happened when they brought him to the hospital and tried to keep him there by force.

' "He went berserk and clawed his brother to the ground and ran off into the night," said the bewildered father. "When the police caught up with him he claimed to be Jesus Christ and at other times Moses."

'I asked the man when it had all begun: "When my son and some of his friends in the technical college were playing ouija." This was becoming a familiar story. I commanded the spirits to leave the boy in Jesus' name. Within five minutes he had returned to normal, much to the amazement of all.'

Mr Tarleton added: 'An irrational feeling of fear, often accompanied by acute depression, is a familiar by-product of this so-called game. It can be intense enough to provoke suicidal tendencies.' This is confirmed by Canon John Pearce-Higgins, former vice-provost of Southwark Cathedral, in London, who claims that several people have tried to take their own lives because of messages received through ouija boards – messages which he considers have very likely come from spirits with a 'lethal sense of humour'. He says that one of these victims, whose life was saved, threw herself in front of a bus so that she could 'join her dead father'.

Comparable cases of malevolent spirits masquerading as those of dead relatives, often being attracted through a ouija board, are recalled by many exorcists.

The Reverend James Song claims he had to fight such a spirit when he was the Vicar of Holy Trinity at Matlock Bath,

Derbyshire. The principal victim was an eighteen-year-old Roman Catholic factory-worker, Peter, who had been playing with a board at home for more than two years. He apparently made contact with a spirit claiming to be that of his dead Uncle George.

Mr Song, now a vicar in Surrey, told me: 'Peter was perfectly at ease with this spirit because it seemed so well-disposed and, of course, because he was convinced it was that of his uncle. That's how spirits of evil often operate. They infiltrate themselves into the confidence of a victim, with messages which seem interesting and encouraging, until they feel secure enough to reveal their real identity.'

This particular spirit, it seems, revealed itself eventually in an unusual way as Peter was preparing for a fishing trip. 'He was alone in the room when he suddenly saw his fishing-tackle moving slowly from one side of the hearth to the other. This so frightened him that he got his rosary and started saying his beads. Then, almost immediately, he felt his neck being seized and twisted violently right around. Later this happened several times – often when I was present. I heard the terrible cricking sound as if his neck was being snapped. I was also there with his father and brother when he was hurled bodily across the room, as if by unseen hands, and on that occasion again I saw how he was being tortured.'

The painful neck-twisting was only part of the torture. It seems that Peter's invisible tormentor was also assaulting him in another way. It was this secondary style of assault which did most to undermine Peter's health and which was to lead, eventually, to him being cleared by exorcism.

Mr Song explained: 'At first, not surprisingly, he was too embarrassed to mention this additional problem to his parents or to his elder brother. He repeatedly had the sensation that there were feathers tickling his genitals. This stimulated him and provoked him into masturbation. That sort of activity is common among young people, but with Peter it was different because of the intensity of the compulsion. Soon he was reaching the stage where he was masturbating about eighteen times a night and at every opportunity during the day. He'd keep hurrying to the lavatory because he was again being aroused by what felt like feathers. After a while he was completely haggard and emaciated but he simply couldn't stop.'

Finally Peter broke down and confided the whole story to his mother. She'd read about Mr Song in the *Daily Mirror* and decided to visit him with Peter.

But was this really a symptom of possession? Or merely one of unrestrained lust? What possible motive could a spirit have for leading a human into such excessive self-abuse?

'This entity inside him was causing him great distress and doing him harm – which is quite common with evil spirits – but in this case there was another reason,' said Mr Song. 'The only way demons can experience human pleasures is through the human body and so, very often, they drive that body into excesses or deviations for their gratification. This thing was drawing pleasure from the sexual excitement it kept stirring in Peter.'

He closely questioned other members of the family and became convinced that there was a spill-over syndrome, that both the other men were being shadowed by spirit-transference. 'The father and the elder son told me they'd been having the same sort of feather-tickling sensations as Peter. They'd also got into a pattern of intense masturbation – something they denied having experienced before the start of Peter's troubles – although they were not being driven to the same degree as Peter. They agreed, however, that the compulsion was constantly growing stronger in both of them and it was obvious to me that the spirit was pleasuring itself vicariously through them.'

The mother was apparently not being directly affected by an alien spirit although the unnatural atmosphere in the home was impinging on her.

Mr Song exorcised the three men and performed a ceremony of spiritual cleansing for the house. He told me: 'I kept in close contact with the family, as I always do after an exorcism, and it was obvious that there was no longer a demon in the house. And Peter was glad to destroy the ouija board.'

The exorcism of the three men was briefer than that required for thirty-two-year-old Phyllis* who, according to Mr Song, was invaded by a group of entities – after she had been indulging in ouija-type behaviour.

Phyllis, a mother of four young children, was married to a lorry driver. Her extraordinary infestation came after a 'game' which many might regard as innocuous but which follows a pattern considered by priests to be dangerous. She discovered that a needle suspended on a thread could divine the sex of a person in a photograph. It would move in circles over a female and in straight lines over a male.

The moving needle was infallible, even if a picture was hidden under a sheet of paper, and Phyllis saw this as a splendid party trick. She used it to baffle and amuse her friends. But the fun started becoming disconcertingly tainted one November evening when she was challenged to demonstrate again over a covered photograph. This time the dangling needle did not move. She went on trying and trying. Still no success. Eventually her friends removed the cover to let her see the picture of an elderly and distinguished-looking man. She tried yet again – letting the needle almost touch the face in the photograph – but still there was no movement. Then they told her that the man had been a doctor. And that he was dead.

'This experience both frightened and fascinated her,' said Mr Song. 'She decided to experiment a bit further and that carried her into deeper danger.'

Alone at home, she arranged the letters of the alphabet in a circle on the dining-room table and willed 'the spirit of the needle' – with the sliver of metal hanging as usual from the thread – to identify itself through some communication. For a while nothing happened. She concentrated harder, convinced there was psychic power within the needle which, with enough determination, she could probably unleash. And she later claimed that eventually, slowly and jerkily at first, the needle began to move. It pointed to one letter after another, in the fashion of a moving glass, to spell the name of the deceased doctor. Now, it seems, the message was coming through faster and apparently with more confidence: 'Trust me . . . do as I say . . . I am your friend and guide.'

'There was a spirit present but it was not that of the doctor and certainly not that of a friend,' says Mr Song. 'It was a roaming entity of evil which had been attracted by her eagerness and vulnerability and which, to win her confidence, was pretending to be benevolent.'

During the following weeks Phyllis had many table-top conversations with the 'spirit of the needle'. She was oblivious to the fact that it was obsessing her and that it was starting to possess her. It gave her information about relatives and friends. It told her, for instance, that one woman living near-by would die on a certain day. Phyllis told the woman's family and they laughed at her for being so stupid. The woman did not appear to be unwell. But she died on the day predicted.

'Many people may regard that sort of power as incredible but it doesn't seem like that to me,' says Mr Song. 'I have encountered evil, real satanic evil, far too often. And that's what was then moving into Phyllis . . .'

By this time the spirit was apparently starting to control Phyllis's life. 'She consulted it about almost everything she did,' said Mr Song. 'She even asked it to advise her on what she should eat. The needle now seemed to have immense energy. It would make the thread writhe and convulse like a snake and it would lead her to the larder. There it would point at the sugar, always at the sugar, which she consumed by the bagful. She was convinced that this guidance was coming from the dead doctor who was now her closest and wisest friend. In time she was eating nothing but sugar, no matter how much her husband tried to make her see sense, and her weight increased from about nine stone to more than fourteen.'

The 'living needle' also dictated her choice of reading. 'She used to take it to the library and let it choose her books. It would arch upwards on its thread and point at those she had to take. They were all in the violence and horror categories . . .'

So it would appear that her days were now spent reading her needle-selected books and consuming more and more of her needle-ordained sugar.

Her attitude towards her family changed. She had been a loving mother and wife but now she was usually morose and often violent. The children were frightened of being with her, never knowing when she might have another savage mood, and the house became neglected and filthy.

Neighbours shunned her after the accurate death prediction, and after predictions of a similar though less dramatic nature, because they were now regarding her as a 'bit of a witch'.

This was how the situation had degenerated when Phyllis's husband despairingly begged help from the family doctor. And it was the doctor who eventually sought the guidance of Mr Song.

Now here, of course, must come the obvious questions which I put to Mr Song: was it not plain that this woman, rather than being possessed, was mentally deranged? Why should it be accepted that she was a victim of psychic evil?

'Naturally I gave careful consideration to the possibility that she might have some clinical mental illness, or that she might merely be acting up in order to be the centre of attention, as I invariably do before deciding that anyone needs exorcism,' replied Mr Song. 'I am extremely cautious about agreeing to conduct these ceremonies for, apart from the fact that I find them emotionally costly to myself, they can do great harm if performed without justification. Some exorcists have tended to barge in without real thought and without reference to God.'

He emphasised that he has a gift for discerning evil and added that he was conscious of it when, with the doctor present, he had his first meeting with Phyllis. 'Everything seemed to indicate that here was a case of demon-possession,' he said. 'But I was still not entirely satisfied. . .'

For two days he prayed until he was confident that Phyllis's only hope lay in exorcism. That, he believed, was the answer from God.

Four lay Christians accompanied him at midday to the small and untidy house where they were joined by the family doctor. The four of them started praying in the dining-room – as they and others were to continue doing through the long hours ahead – while Mr Song and the doctor went into the next room with Phyllis.

'The doctor is a committed Christian and he joined me in prayer,' said Mr Song. 'Usually when I pray for a person in these circumstances demon-possession eventually manifests itself and the person goes into a state of trance.'

That is what happened to Phyllis. She was relaxed in her armchair, her jaw slack and her eyes half-shut. Mr Song stood close to her and spoke firmly to the entity, or entities, with which he believed her to be infested: 'In the name of Jesus I command you to tell me who you are!'

A gruff male voice, quite unlike that of the woman, replied loudly: 'My name is Pluto.'

To the ancient Greeks Pluto was the God of the Dead. Mr Song believes that, by the time the need for exorcism is recognised, there is usually more than one demon present. 'One gets in and then attracts others, rather in the way that human squatters do in a house, and it is imperative to drive them all out.'

He continued his dialogue with the presumed demon: 'I command you to tell me how many of you there are in this person!'

There was no immediate response and he repeated the order. The same male voice told him, with what seemed to be a boasting of strength, that there were fourteen.

Now Mr Song felt he had a clear insight into the magnitude of the task ahead. He prayed silently and braced himself for the start of the contest: 'Pluto . . . I command you to leave Phyllis in the name of Jesus and to go back to Gehenna [Greek for Hell] where you belong!'

Suddenly the woman, who had seemed almost unconscious, jerked upright and burst into a frenzy of violence. Words of abuse came torrenting from her, all in that strange and mocking male voice, and she tried to rake her finger-nails down Mr Song's face. He stepped back, startled, and she snatched up a near-by Bible which she tried to rip apart. She bared her teeth in menace like a crazed and cornered animal and then she badly bit her tongue. The two of them held her down while the doctor gave her a tranquilliser. 'He told me the injection was strong enough to knock an ordinary man out for several hours,' says Mr Song. 'But it didn't have that effect on Phyllis. It subdued her temporarily but she was back to normal within twenty minutes.'

As she recovered full consciousness, the entity calling itself Pluto had gone. Its place in the 'front line' now appeared to have been taken by another spirit which, in a very different masculine voice, introduced itself as Death.

Mr Song likens the exorcism of a multiplicity of demons to the peeling of an onion. 'You get rid of one skin and then expose another. Then under this is yet another and so on until you reach the core.'

The demon calling itself Death changed the atmosphere around them: 'The whole room was filled with a sickly sweet smell – the sort of smell one would associate with a dead body.' There was also another striking change in Phyllis. Sometimes she would be producing that strange voice, yelling obscenities and threats, and then she would revert to her own voice – as though Phyllis, the real Phyllis, was consciously joining in this battle for supremacy. She was desperately frightened. That was obvious from her tone and, during those brief moments when she was in control, from the expression on her face. She claimed to be seeing her own corpse floating away in a white coffin and she was begging to be saved. Then it seemed that she was again being pushed into the background and the room was again resounding with the taunting words of Death.

'When I finally exorcised this spirit, which was particularly tenacious, Phyllis literally fell down just as if she had died. I kept patting her face and telling her to wake up. Then she opened her eyes and acted as if she'd just come out of a deep but normal sleep. She wasn't in the slightest distressed and, although I refrained from questioning her, I had the impression that she remembered nothing of what had just been happening.'

The struggle with Death, which had reached its climax at mid-afternoon, had taken a severe toll on Mr Song. Weariness made him feel despairingly inadequate. He was sure there were still twelve demons, possibly ones even more determined and dangerous, and suddenly he felt he could no longer continue. He knelt beside Phyllis and prayed. He prayed for guidance, protection and strength. 'Very soon there seemed to be a radiant brightness in the room. My strength and confidence were restored for I knew then that Jesus was with me.'

The group in the adjoining room, relieved at times by other members of Mr Song's congregation, continued to pray as he and the doctor worked on through the night. And the demons which he says became manifest, each with a distinctive voice, displayed an astounding range of garish peculiarities. Possibly the most revolting of all was one which in the early hours of the morning transformed Phyllis into a snake. 'Her appearance changed in the most remarkable manner,' says Mr Song. 'She was squirming and writhing around the floor on her stomach, her eyes bulging like organ stops, and she seemed to have taken on the physical characteristics of a snake.'

During some of these sessions of acute manifestation she again became violent, displaying great physical strength, and she suffered a series of small injuries. They repeatedly dabbed away the blood.

'It was essential for her, as for all the people I exorcise, to place her faith in Christ for cleansing, salvation and protection,' says Mr Song. 'But the responsibilities of a priest continue long after the completion of an exorcism. After-care is vital for, apart from the danger of reinfection, people who have suffered so deeply are likely to feel very insecure. So the doctor and I ministered to her and watched her progress through the next few months. And she was soon back to leading a normal and healthy life – although she had been well on the road to destruction.'

* * *

* * *

The first of Phyllis's fourteen demons introduced itself with these words: 'My name is Pluto.'

It may seem fortuitously convenient that this entity should have been encountered by an exorcist with a sound grasp of Greek mythology. Many exorcists would know Pluto only as a planet or as a comic-cartoon dog. Would they have received a different reply? Was the one given to Mr Song just a little *too* convenient? I feel that is the case.

This does not mean I am challenging Mr Song's memory or his integrity. Nor am I attempting to belittle the value of his work. I know of the high esteem with which he is regarded by his contemporaries and I recognise the help he has given to the spiritually afflicted.

What I do suggest is that he and many other exorcists tend to put too much importance on names which may be supplied by possessing entities. This group of presumed demons, it would seem, lied convincingly to Phyllis. They persuaded her they were all part of one spirit – that of the doctor in the photograph. Their motive, presumably, was to play on her emotions, to make her react as they wished. Would it not be logical then, if this were true, for them to respond with similar deceit to Mr Song – for them to regard his weak spot as a target?

Mr Song has admitted that he is usually frightened when in the proximity of evil. So any alien intelligence, when being challenged by him, would surely attempt to capitalise on that fear – building it in every possible way in order to unnerve him and beat him. It would seem that the name Pluto – like that of Death – was given merely to increase his dread.

Exorcists, after all, insist that such entities represent the Prince of Liars.

* * *
* * *

Ouija boards are used by many families in an attempt to ease the pain of bereavement. They try to call back the spirits of loved ones and, exorcists warn, they are exposing themselves to great psychic risks.

One of the strangest cases I have investigated happened in Exeter.

Shortly after six o'clock on a dank evening in January 1975 a twenty-five-year-old builder, Richard Johnson,* was at home chatting with his young stepdaughter, Carol. His wife, Sylvia, was in the kitchen preparing a meal and her elder daughter, Jean, was out posting a letter. Richard was wearing a chunky purple sweater and old grey slacks and was relaxing after work in his favourite armchair near the window. It was a low and rather shabby chair, covered in dark red fabric which he had invariably used since moving into the house only four months earlier on 27 September 1974, just after his marriage. Carol has described how he was speaking quietly and tenderly to her, as he had done so often before, but this time the circumstances were very different.

Richard Johnson had been dead for seven weeks. He had been killed almost instantaneously in a road accident near Plymouth on 6 December 1974.

Carol apparently accepted his presence without surprise or fear – cheerfully answering his questions just as she had done when he was alive. 'He smiled a lot and seemed happy and I didn't see any marks of the accident,' she said later. She found his visit reassuring for, like her mother, she regarded it as yet another development in a comforting and benevolent haunting.

Sylvia Johnson is convinced that her husband's spirit lingered in the house for months after his funeral because of love which transcended the grave. There was a pointer to this, she believes, in a promise he had made just before their wedding.

Sylvia was fourteen years older than Richard and had secured a divorce after her first husband went away with another woman. Her daughters were aged five and eleven when she remarried and Richard, knowing the insecurity she had suffered, had then said: 'From now on you and the girls have got me. I'll always look after you.'

Sylvia says: 'The girls adored Richard because, unlike their real father, he gave them genuine affection. There was a particularly strong bond between him and little Carol. She'd be on his lap for twenty minutes or more most evenings, almost as soon as he'd got back from work, giggling and chattering with him. He had just a few grey hairs and she used to forage for them and pull them out. He had incredible patience.'

That happiness lasted less than three months. On the first Friday in December Richard had been working just outside Plymouth and was on his way back to Exeter. Visibility was bad. There was a crash involving a heavy mechanical digger. The other men in the car were injured. Only Richard Johnson was killed.

'Suddenly I heard a curious rustling sound from the conservatory at the back of the house,' said Sylvia. 'It was so loud that I hurried to investigate but it stopped as soon as I opened the door and there was nothing to be seen.'

An hour later she was given the news. Her husband had died just before she had stepped into the conservatory.

What happens to a person's spirit at the moment of death? Information said to have been gathered at seances, much of it on tape, provides the basis for many theories. One of the most commonly-held is that the spirits of the newly-dead, particularly of those who had died unexpectedly and violently, often have difficulty in accepting that they have been torn from earthly life. It is believed that although they can see their own bodies, as objects quite detached from them, they are too shocked and confused to grasp the reality of their deaths. According to the theory, they then struggle to step back into the world of the living – drawn by their old desires or ambitions and, in many cases, by their deep concern for those who are left to grieve. The length of their struggles, it is argued, can not be measured in terms of time as we understand it. The eternity beyond death is timeless.

Many spirits, according to mediums, understand their new state in what we would regard as seconds. They may not be reconciled to it, however, and they may then strive to project themselves into the consciousness of the living, particularly into that of people with whom they had a close attachment, in their efforts to demonstrate that they still exist.

Truly selfless love is regarded as spiritual – as a quality which does not die with the physical body. It is said to live on in the released spirit which then, longing to be near and to comfort, can sometimes communicate through an atmosphere or some physical manifestation. So was that rustling in Sylvia Johnson's conservatory really caused by Richard's spirit? She does not claim to know and, although she was 'vaguely aware of his presence', there was nothing more to suggest that he might have returned to the house – until nearly two weeks later.

A few days before Christmas, late in the afternoon, five-year-old Carol was playing alone in her room when, she says, she suddenly saw 'Richard all in sunshine'. On that first occasion, apparently, he did not speak but he was smiling and she was not in the least alarmed by his presence. The feelings she vividly remembers were of excitement and delight. She ran to the door and called down to her mother: 'Quick – come here! Richard's in my room!'

Her tone was so insistent that Sylvia and Jean hurried up the stairs and across the landing. Carol was just inside her door, pointing and staring in wonderment at the far corner. 'Look!' she said. 'Richard's here . . . he's really here!'

There was nothing for them to see. Only the furniture and the rose-patterned wallpaper and the watercolours in white frames. 'Up there!' persisted Carol. 'He's all in sunshine!' She was now looking at a spot high up the wall. Still they could see nothing.

'We told her not to be silly,' says Sylvia Johnson. 'I put my arms around her and explained that Richard couldn't be there because he was in Heaven. She kept pointing at the wall and arguing with me because she couldn't understand why I wasn't able to see him as well. Then, suddenly, she was very upset because she could no longer see him. She kept staring at that spot of the wall as if trying to puzzle out where he'd gone.

'I took her downstairs and cuddled her, trying to soothe her and convince her she'd made a mistake, but all the time I felt oddly guilty. I hadn't seen Richard and neither had Jean, and yet I had a strong feeling, one I couldn't rationalise, that he had been with us in that room. I'd sensed his presence and, although I'd kept up an act for Carol's sake, I'd welcomed it. I kept thinking about the promise he'd made and that night, alone in bed, I was convinced that he was keeping that promise.' She claims that two weeks later she too saw her dead husband. 'He must have been making a supreme effort to reach me because on more than one occasion I'd felt a hand gently patting my shoulder. The sensation was so strong that I spoke to him, tried to draw him closer, but there was no reply. There was a warmth and an atmosphere of well-being in the house and the three of us accepted that Richard was watching over us and protecting us. Then one day he did manage to appear to me. He didn't say anything but just smiled and nodded his head. I stepped towards him, wanting to embrace him, but suddenly he was gone.'

Carol now started seeing her stepfather quite regularly. He never manifested himself again to Sylvia, or ever to Jean, but he had a special rapport with Carol.

'Jean and I could never hear or see him but, after a while, that didn't bother Carol,' says Sylvia. 'She could obviously see him there in his red chair and, if we happened to be in the room, she would ignore us and speak to him quite unself-consciously.'

These phantom sessions usually lasted three or four minutes. They usually ended abruptly with Carol explaining: 'Richard said he had to go.'

'I didn't feel any need to seek help from the church because I saw nothing worrying in what was happening,' says Sylvia. 'It wasn't doing Carol any harm and it was a great relief to know for sure that Richard was still with us. I was very grateful.'

In the autumn of 1975 the family moved to a semi-detached house in a different part of the city and it seems that the spirit of Richard moved with them. He apparently still sat in the red chair, which Carol now insisted on having in her bedroom, but his visits became less frequent. There would be gaps of weeks, sometimes of a month or more, without any sign of him. Eventually, towards the end of 1977, he seemed to have gone altogether. It was as if he was finally satisfied that the family was secure and that his work was done. Sylvia then started to experience great loneliness. She felt that she had been abandoned. She wanted Richard back. She needed him. And it was Jean, then aged fifteen, who suggested a solution. Perhaps they could contact Richard through a ouija board. Perhaps they could ask him to return.

Commercially-produced ouija boards have all the letters of the alphabet together with the words 'yes' and 'no' around the perimeter. All those involved in an attempt to summon spirits place a finger lightly on a triangle of wood whilst collectively willing a spirit to make its presence known. Eventually, if they are successful, the wooden triangle begins to move, spelling out names and messages by aiming at one letter after another. It is as if a spirit has entered the triangle and is conversing through it. Some people suspect that the movements are possibly caused by a prankster at the table, one who is deliberately steering the triangle, or that they are generated by the collective unconscious thoughts of the group. These may be the causes in some instances but my researches have convinced me that the energy is often that of a psychic entity.

Such entities display a wide-ranging intelligence and a willingness to answer spoken questions. The words 'yes' and 'no' are on the board to speed question-and-answer sessions.

The triangle may identify the controlling spirit, for instance, by spelling the name 'William'. The spokesman at the table may then ask: 'William, are you related to someone present in this room?' The triangle will then move to 'yes' or 'no'.

'William, did you live in London?'

The triangle may then move to 'yes' or it may start to spell a place name.

So more and more information is obtained through a series of questions and answers.

Many groups use a simplified version, with the triangle being replaced by an upturned drinking-glass and the letters being on cards placed around a table, but Jean Johnson had a real ouija board.

Sylvia was reluctant to use it. She had read warnings about ouija and was nervous about dabbling with the unknown. Jean eventually took the initiative in November 1978 when – without Sylvia's knowledge – she tried to summon Richard's spirit while staying at the home of a schoolfriend.

Both girls insist that they did attract an entity which claimed to be Richard. Jean described her mother's unhappiness and asked this entity to enter her own home. There seemed to be some conflict, some psychic clash of wills, before the spirit agreed. Jean then telephoned her mother in jubilation and told her to be ready. Richard was coming home.

Carol was also away, spending a few days with relatives, and Sylvia went to her room where she sat in the red chair. She concentrated on Richard, forming mental pictures of him and willing him to come to her. She pleaded aloud: 'Richard, I need you . . . I need you so much. Please come back to me.' Nothing happened and eventually, exhausted, she went to bed.

The following day Jean returned and she was adamant that Richard, through the ouija board, had given a firm promise. He needed help to reach them, she insisted, and they had to give him that help.

Sylvia wanted to believe and that was why, despite her anxieties, she allowed herself to be persuaded. They sat at a table, just the two of them, and used a glass in their attempts to reach him. And, like Phyllis with her needle, they got a response. There seemed to be an entity present which, answering their questions accurately, appeared to have an intimate knowledge of their lives. Sylvia was convinced by then that this was the spirit of her dead husband and she pleaded with it not to leave.

'It said that it belonged with us and that it would stay for ever,' says Jean. 'Suddenly, for no reason at all, mum threw her head back and started laughing ever so loud in a weird way. I was terrified. She was cackling and staring like someone gone mad. I'd never seen her like it before and I knew that something awful had happened.'

Sylvia's memories of the next few hours are a hopeless jumble. She can recall being filled with fear, a more terrible fear than she'd ever known, but she can remember nothing of her strange laughter or her irrational behaviour. Then she returned to normality. Or, rather, almost to normality. She was again in control of herself and she could think clearly. But she had a deep and inexplicable sense of foreboding: 'I seemed to be living, emotionally, in a grey cloud. It was as if I was waiting for some inevitable disaster.'

There was no disaster. But soon there were disturbing happenings. She is very much a woman of habit and every night for many years she'd wound her watch and put it on her bedside table. One morning she discovered it was no longer there. She found it on a low bookcase. Other small objects were moved in a similar fashion. One evening they noticed that the back door, which had been locked and bolted, was wide open. This is a style of phenomenon familiar to exorcists who regard it as a basic flaunting of power by an occupying spirit. There are dangers, they say, that this power will start being demonstrated more violently.

'Some people might feel that I'd become absent-minded or plain stupid,' said Sylvia. 'But it wasn't that way at all. There was something very wrong in our home and the atmosphere always seemed heavily unpleasant.'

She rang an Anglican clergyman, a family friend living in London, who said prayers with her on the telephone – and who suggested that she should seek help locally from the Liberal Catholic priest, John Wheaton. He knew Father Wheaton well and, although there were certain differences in their beliefs, he respected his authority as an exorcist.

Father Wheaton exorcised and blessed the house on 15 November 1978 and, a couple of weeks later, he held a Requiem Mass for the soul of Richard Johnson.

Sylvia regained her health and became, once again, a fit and self-possessed woman. 'I still like to think that Richard is watching over us,' she said. 'But I know he's no longer on this earth and I don't need to see him. He has shown me conclusively that there is life after death and I know that I'll be with him again – when the right time comes.'

There is a tendency among many priests to categorise all 'ouija invaders' as demons. Father Wheaton takes a different view. 'The word "demon" is used far too loosely – possibly because it has a fine dramatic ring,' he says. 'Demonic possession does happen, of course, but it is extremely rare. The idea of us being constantly surrounded by a horde of demons, all jostling to get inside us, cannot be supported. Most of the entities attracted through ouija are elementals – very low and primitive intelligences which are amoral rather than evil. In many ways they are rather like the playful puppies of the spirit world, having no awareness of right or wrong, and they can cause a great deal of disruption and distress.'

My investigations have convinced me that there are great dangers in ouija, with participants exposed to the possibility of emotional or psychological damage. Large numbers of dabblers have been apparently unscathed and this is why there is a tendency to ignore warnings or to dismiss them as being gross exaggerations. Many who play with ouija boards point out that they have done so before and have never come to harm. This is rather like a man walking bare-footed through a patch of grass known to be infested with adders. Chances are high that he will be lucky enough not to get bitten. He may do the walk several times until he convinces himself, and possibly others, that there really is no risk. But his behaviour is still placing him in jeopardy.

As long ago as 1968 the magazine *Psychic News* was urging the Minister of Health to consider banning the sale of ouija boards to children. Their letter said: 'Where the ouija board differs from other toys is that the result of the "game" is completely unpredictable. It can be used as a short cut to the subconscious. This has horrifying possibilities. The harm that can be done to a child's mind by the messages which are spelt out is incalculable.'

Why was *Psychic News* concerned only about children? Adults are also vulnerable.

Much of the 'ouija backlash' unquestionably does stem from the subconscious of the participants – often being aggravated by individual or group hysteria – but there is enough evidence to suggest that ouija offers far more than 'a short cut to the subconscious'.

Major stores in Britain have now stopped selling ouija, but boards can still be bought by mail-order. One catalogue describes a ouija-table as 'a vastly improved version of the ouija board'. The same organisation offers a range of equipment, tapes and books – nearly all of which seem calculated to encourage experiments with the occult. One of the tapes is claimed to contain the rites of traditional witchcraft and the sales-blurb reads: 'Ideal for anyone wishing to form a coven but unable to make contact with an established group. The rites can also be easily adapted for solo practise.'

The blurb of *The Devil's Prayer Book* promises that 'all the rituals, tools, spells, etc., used by modern witchcraft covens are dealt with, giving full texts'. It adds: 'The author chose to remain anonymous after receiving threats from various witches who did not want him to publish the book.' That is obviously nonsense, just bait for the gullible. It implies that the 'various witches' who are alleged to have threatened the author – knowing he was planning to publish – are too stupid to deduce that this is his work.

But what of the information in the books and tapes?

The leader of one witch coven gives this opinion: 'We regard much of this stuff as rather paltry but some of it is potent and, in the wrong hands, it could cause trouble.'

The man running this mail-order organisation told me: 'Our policy is to meet the needs of all people without any form of censorship and, particularly in the last two or three years, we've seen an increasing demand for our material.'

That material, I feel, is helping to fan the increasing need for exorcism. There should be legislation to outlaw this mail-order trade in ouija.

5 Intruders from the grave

Carol Johnson is adamant that she had regular conversations with her dead stepfather. Her evidence might well be challenged, however, as being the product of a child's lively imagination. Many people would dismiss her version as fantasy, for few issues have divided Christians more severely than that of communication between the living and the dead.

There are three broad attitudes: first, that such communication is possible but dangerous; second, that it is possible and of great potential value – in bringing comfort to the bereaved and in helping with the diagnosis of spiritual problems; and third, that it is patent nonsense and those who claim to practise it are either fools or charlatans.

Each of these views has a bearing on an individual's thinking about exorcism. The first opinion was endorsed in 1926 by Lord William Gascoyne Cecil, Bishop of Exeter: 'It is most unwise to attempt to communicate with those who have passed from us. I do not believe that such communication is impossible. It may be quite possible, but we have no guarantee whatever that we are, in fact, communicating with our friends.

'In the spiritual world beyond the grave there must be an intelligence, probably greater than that which we possess, and that intelligence will not permit any insolent commands to spirits to wait or communicate at the will of human beings, but will require on the other hand that those guilty of presumption should be severely punished.

'It may well be that the fitting punishment for such disorder is that these presumptuous inquiries should be handed over to malign spirits, who amuse themselves by giving information which is false and which tends to humiliate . . . '

Controversy was then simmering between religious leaders on the subject of the occult – a word derived from the Latin *occultus*, meaning secret or hidden – and nine years later, in 1937, a major inquiry was initiated by the Church of England. The Archbishop of Canterbury, Dr Cosmo Lang, appointed a committee of ten – chaired by the Bishop of Bath and Wells, the Right Reverend Francis Underhill – to investigate spiritualism and other forms of psychic phenomena.

Their investigations lasted two years and their findings were considered so disturbing that the Archbishop decided the report should not be published.

It fell under the forty-year embargo controlling archepiscopal documents and was deposited in the archives at Lambeth Palace. It was regarded as one of the Church's most closely-guarded secrets until 1979 – after all members of the committee had died – when its contents were made public. They showed that most of the researchers had accepted that there was evidence of communication with discarnate spirits and that some of the practices of spiritualism might 'add a new immediacy and richness' to the traditional Christian belief in the Communion of Saints.

This was a devastating blow to priests who thunder against any attempts at necromancy, particularly as it had the approval of men highly regarded in the Church, including Dean Matthews of St Paul's and Canon Harold Anson, Master of the Temple. They were among the committee members impressed by several of the claims made by spiritualists, and the majority had concluded that there were 'quite clear parallels' between certain modern phenomena and the miraculous events recorded in the Gospels.

All this helped to confirm a view expressed in 1976 by the Bishop of Southwark, Dr Mervyn Stockwood, in his diocesan review:

> Even if I were not a Christian, my studies would incline me to believe in a dimension of reality that is beyond what are normally regarded as the limits of human experience. Clairvoyance, clair-audience, communication between the

living and the dead should not be treated as disreputable words in the dictionary of the spiritualist. Not only do they give rise to phenomena that have been carefully studied by students of psychical research but they are to be found, though expressed differently, in Holy Scriptures. It is my personal belief that each of us has a physical body and a spiritual or counterpart body disengages itself from the physical and continues to exist as the medium of our personality in a new dimension.

Most amateurs use variations of ouija when trying to attract these 'spiritual or counterpart bodies' and, as we have seen, the sequels can be horrifying. Professional spiritualists consider that their trance techniques provide a safer and far more effective method for attracting the spirits of the dead. However, many priests claim that spiritualists are also often fooled over the identity of summoned spirits and that there is a danger of them failing to detect 'unwanted trespassers'. They argue that, in trying to attract the human dead, they can inadvertently open the psychic sluice-gates and so allow entry to other entities which may be mischievous or even dangerously evil. These entities may then linger with them, unrecognised, and contaminate them and those with whom they come in contact. Friends and members of their families, it is believed, can suffer from this invisible spill-over.

Father John Tracy suspects that was the cause of a mystery which brought fear to a home in Chapel Street, London. He is one of the Jesuits at the Farm Street Church of the Immaculate Conception near London's Berkeley Square and his help was sought at eleven o'clock at night by a distraught young man.

'He had two large dogs and he came with what seemed to me like a very strange story. He said he'd been in the house on his own while his mother, a woman I happen to know, was out for the evening. He was coming down the stairs when a plank of wood, about three feet in length, suddenly hurtled upwards past his head. It had gone right up the stairs and then landed with a clatter on the landing. This terrified him so much that he called the dogs and rushed straight out of the house.

'I asked if he'd been drinking or taking drugs and it was clear that he hadn't. It was also clear that he was still very shaken and afraid. One of the things that impressed me was that he was obviously trying to tell the truth without any embellishments. I asked him if he'd noticed any odd behaviour on the part of the dogs. If he'd been trying to sensationalise things he'd have been tempted to say they'd been howling or had shown some other sign of fear. But, no, there had been nothing unusual about the dogs. Because I was sufficiently convinced that he was genuinely scared I offered to go home with him and to bless the house and stay there until his mother returned.'

When they arrived the man took Father Tracy to see the plank on the landing. 'But when he saw it he was even more bewildered and agitated. He kept insisting that it had moved again, that it wasn't where it had fallen, although no one else had been in the building.'

In another part of the house Father Tracy, by then exploring on his own, found a gap in some wooden panelling.

'The plank fitted it exactly but I could see no way in which it could have been moved to where we found it. And I certainly could not explain how it could have gone shooting up the stairs of its own volition.'

Near that gap in the panelling he discovered another peculiarity. 'I suddenly walked into a cold spot – a square block of instant iciness about three feet square. It was like stepping into a butcher's deep-freeze. I was so puzzled that I experimented a few times – stepping in and out of the coldness – but I could not work out why there was such a dramatic difference in the temperature.'

Another man who was spending a few days there as a guest arrived back just as Father Tracy had finished blessing the house.

'I asked him if he'd noticed anything odd about the place but he said he hadn't. Then he told me a bit about himself and he mentioned that his own mother was one of the three top mediums in Britain.'

Coincidence? Possibly. But it is equally possible, surely, that some spill-over entity had become attached to the guest, that he had unwittingly carried it like a virus into the house.

The phenomenon reported by the young man was comparatively mild but it could be of significance. Other cases have indicated that small ripples of psychic disturbance, sometimes so slight that they can almost be ignored, can precede events of a far more devastating nature.

* * *
* * *

Problems can also erupt after spiritualists have apparently been successful in contacting the human dead. Father Robert Brunswick, one of the Church of England's official advisers on exorcism in the Diocese of Liverpool, says this happened after a seance was arranged in a local church.

The vicar and members of his congregation had become convinced that this church was haunted by a 'troubled spirit'. Powerful smells would fill the church regularly during services and they always followed a pattern. First there would be a fragrance of flowers which would then be displaced by the stench of rotting flesh.

Father Brunswick told me that 'eventually this incumbent decided on action which was completely out of order. He asked a woman spiritualist to conduct a seance in the church and invited three others, including a Church Army captain, to be present as observers. I know these guests who are intelligent and responsible people – ones whose testimony can be trusted – and they have reported exactly what happened. The spiritualist got them all to sing "Rock of Ages" and, while they were doing so, a briefcase full of books was picked up from the floor of the chancel and flung about eighty feet against the wall at the back of the church. It was too heavy to have been thrown that distance by any of them there and, anyway, not one of them had touched it. Then the voice of the spiritualist, who was still singing, dropped several octaves until it sounded like that of a croaky old man.'

The Church Army captain, perturbed by this change of voice, shouted towards the spiritualist: 'Who are you?'

She replied in the voice of an elderly male, 'Sam, I am looking for . . .' The rest of the words were incoherent and then the woman burst into tears. That was the end of the seance.

'It all seemed very inconclusive because none of them could think of anyone called Sam,' said Father Brunswick. 'During the next few days, however, the vicar made inquiries. He discovered that about ten years earlier, long before he'd moved to the parish, a verger had died while on his way to get the church ready for a Sunday service. His name was Sam.'

Sam had apparently been a conscientious man who had loved the church and who would have felt guilty if he had ever failed to complete his duties. He had failed, of course, on the day of his death. Is it not possible, then, that such a feeling of guilt might have transcended the grave? Is it not conceivable that Sam's spirit was drawn to the church, restless and unhappy, because he had left his work unfinished?

What is particularly curious here is the throwing of the briefcase. That would seem an action quite out of keeping with the character of Sam. Was this, again, a prelude to more possible violence?

'The seance, of course, should never had been permitted, for necromancy is totally condemned by the Church,' said Father Brunswick. 'Unfortunately, there are still priests who, possibly because they are ignorant of the dangers, dabble in spiritualism. I reported this case to the Bishop and I doubt if that vicar will repeat his mistake.'

The church was exorcised by Father Brunswick and there were no further manifestations.

* * *
* * *

Records kept by exorcists indicate that spirits of the human dead can cause disruption in homes and also distort the minds of the living – without having been invited by spiritualists or through variations of ouija. In many cases, it is believed, these spirits are tethered to earth by powerful emotions such as possessiveness – which may be concentrated on individuals or on objects.

A typical case of such 'trespassing' was resolved by Father

Brunswick at a house in Speke. 'I was called there because of what seemed like poltergeist activity involving china figurines. They would appear to jump off low shelves and land, very gently, in the lap of the woman living there. This had been going on for nearly eighteen months. Later, while I was getting into the car, I suddenly felt an excruciating pain in the side of my head and it wasn't until later that I understood its significance. It was similar to the pain which the woman's sister, also resident in the house, had suffered before her death of a brain tumour, eighteen months earlier.'

He discovered that the figurines moved when the woman's small daughter went near them and that they belonged to the dead woman. 'In fact, they'd been among her most treasured possessions and she'd always been worried that the child might play with them and break them. I'd come across situations of this type before and I was satisfied that the deceased's spirit was still concerned for the figurines, that she was trying to protect them by passing them to her sister.'

The family confirmed that the figurines did not move again after the exorcism.

A far more horrifying ordeal was inflicted on Joyce Pettigrew* by a possessive spirit. When she was in her late fifties she was invaded by the spirit of her husband's first wife – a woman who, before her sudden and unexpected death, had been domineering, self-centred and obsessively jealous. That was in March 1978 and during the following three years Mrs Pettigrew was driven to the edge of a mental collapse. She had almost uncontrollable urges to attack her husband, to humiliate him and cause great pain. Yet it seemed so baffling, so frighteningly crazy, for she was deeply in love with him.

Howard Pettigrew is one of those self-effacing people who radiate good-natured serenity. He is a retired professional man, immensely polite and considerate, who has a lively interest in music. He is in complete contrast to Joyce's first husband, who died of alcoholism after years of erratic behaviour.

At their home near Sidmouth in Devon, she described to me how, since her childhood, she had never known real love and security until she met Howard. 'This man gave me everything I ever wanted, yet there was this awful thing inside me, goading me into causing him misery.'

This 'thing' was later identified as Bridget, the phantom of the first Mrs Pettigrew. Howard Pettigrew's marriage to Bridget had been turbulent and unhappy. It lasted for thirty-five years only because of his tolerance and forgiving nature. Bridget invariably had her own way in everything, demolishing any opposition with screaming tantrums, and her extravagances strained their finances.

At first he was reluctant to talk freely about this period of his life, for he is a devout Methodist and he considered it un-Christian to denigrate the dead. After a while he gave me the full story. 'But I'm doing so for one reason. I feel it's important that other people should fully understand the problem we've had here. There may be others who are suffering in a similar way and I'd like them to know that they can be helped.'

His home town is in the north of England, where he and Bridget, together with their three children, lived all their married life.

'She was a rather forceful woman who always had to be the centre of attention,' he said eventually. 'For a long time I was running an amateur operatic group and she used to insist on always being cast in the best roles. She did have a good voice but so did some of the other members. I never dared let any of them have a part that she wanted, even if they were more suitable, because then there'd be terrible troubles at home. She was often having awful rows over silly little things with our friends. Once when we were going out for a special dinner with another couple and she suddenly decided that the other woman's fur cape looked better than her own, she ordered the woman to take it off and leave it behind. The woman did as she was told because she knew it didn't do to upset my wife.'

The following day, to keep the peace, he bought a more expensive cape for Bridget. 'I know it must sound weak and stupid but there were also the children to consider and, if I didn't do that sort of thing, the atmosphere in the house would become unbearable.'

Occasionally Bridget would decide, apparently on the spur of the moment, to go away on her own for short holidays. 'She'd never tell me where she was going because she said it was none of my business. Yet she used to get furious when I went out in the evening to attend some meeting to do with the church. I tried to explain that the meetings were important but she always concluded, "Oh . . . go to hell." It's fair to say, I suppose, that she treated me more like her property than her husband . . .'

In 1972 he and Bridget had a holiday in Sidmouth. 'She fell in love with the town and so did I. We walked along the seafront and had this daydream about how it would be wonderful, one day, to retire near here. We were so serious about it that we went round all the estate agents to see the sort of home we might buy.'

That daydream ended in January 1975, a few weeks after Howard Pettigrew retired. Bridget had seen her doctor because of pains in her stomach. Tests showed that she had cancer. She died during an emergency operation.

'I could hardly believe it because it was so sudden,' he said. 'She'd always seemed so fit.'

The following year he moved into a flat near the sea at Sidmouth. From the windows of his sitting-room he could see the promenade where he had once walked with Bridget.

In October 1977 he met Joyce for the first time. She had the seat next to him on a coach day-drip to Cornwall. A week later they had dinner together and in March 1978 they were married. Joyce moved into his flat where, within three days, she was to become apparently possessed by the jealous spirit of his first wife.

Howard had gone to the library that morning and Joyce was alone in the flat. 'Suddenly I had the strangest feeling that I was no longer on my own, that there was someone with me in the kitchen, and I had an overwhelming sensation of depression. It was a dreadful feeling but there didn't seem to be any reason for it. I *had* been happy until that moment. . . . '

That was the moment when she was being entered by the alien spirit. Outside there was the bright sunshine of early spring and, through the open window, there were the reassuring noises of normality. She could hear the rhythmic sound of a neighbour's lawnmower and, from a few gardens away, the laughter of children. Yet here, in the neatness of her kitchen, it seemed that she was being possessed by a woman who was dead. The name 'Bridget' started hammering through her mind.

'It was as though I could hear it, time after time after time, although I wasn't hearing it with my ears. Then I felt very faint.'

Some psychologists might be tempted to give an instant diagnosis. Joyce Pettigrew owed her newly-found happiness to the premature death of another woman. She had usurped the rightful place of that woman. She was being deluded by her own emotions and was very likely inflicting self-punishment for what she subconsciously regarded as her own guilt. But they would have difficulty in explaining the symptoms which were soon to erupt.

Howard Pettigrew has confirmed that, at that stage, he had told Joyce very little about Bridget. He had certainly not discussed Bridget's disturbing behaviour and Joyce knew virtually nothing about her true nature.

During the following weeks Joyce's personality went through a curious change. So did her attitude to Howard. 'I still loved him, but it was as if there was another part of me that hated him, that wanted to wound him. It wanted him to be brought down to his knees. There was an awful battle going on inside me. I kept on being angry with him and full of resentment. Yet I couldn't understand why. I wanted to be close to him, to be a normal loving wife, but at the same time I wanted to scream at him and tell him to clear off.'

It was as if the spirit of Bridget was wreaking vengeance on her husband she had used but not loved – and on the woman who had taken her place in the 'retirement daydream'. It was as if Bridget, unable to accept her own death, was striving to regain her old place as the domineering wife.

Tensions began to develop between Joyce and Howard. She was hearing the insidious promptings of Bridget more and more and her mental turmoil, which she was still trying to stifle, grew enormously when he took her on a visit to his old home town.

They went to a concert there one evening, at a theatre where Bridget had occasionally starred as a solo singer, and Joyce collapsed during the performance. 'First I had a terrible pain in my stomach and then a tightness in my chest. I remember holding my stomach and crying out with the pain and then I went all faint. . . .'

She keeled forward in her seat and was carried out of the auditorium. Outside she recovered quickly with no pain or discomfort to her body, and the local doctor could find no reason for her collapse. The atmosphere in the theatre had not been oppressive. The incident was dismissed as 'one of those things'. But after that evening there was one more difference in Joyce Pettigrew. She had shared her husband's enjoyment of singing and had been an enthusiastic member of a choir for some years, but now she was no longer able to sing.

Bridget had prided herself on her singing. Was she now preventing her successor from having that sort of pleasure? That question did not cross anyone's mind at the time.

'Now I'm sure that's exactly what happened,' she told me. 'Bridget was making it impossible for me to sing – because she could no longer do so and because she was filled with jealousy.'

They moved from the flat to their present home. Joyce continued to deteriorate. Her feelings towards Howard were still on that bewildering seesaw but she never wanted him to leave her on her own in the home because, for the first time in her adult life, she was frightened of being alone. She was a woman who, until shortly before she had met Howard, had held a responsible job as an executive. She was intelligent and practical. Yet she was frightened of something unseen and intangible. However, it was a physical disability which eventually paved the way to her being saved.

Doctors could do little for the arthritis which was slowly starting to cripple her and she decided to seek the help of a well-known faith healer, but without success. After a long session, he told her, 'I can't get through to you as I should like to. I have the sensation that there is someone on your back.' He advised her to consult a woman medium. Howard took her to see the medium in June 1981. She was told then that she was not going insane, as she had now started to fear, but that she was being manipulated by another intelligence.

The only thing they told the medium was that Joyce had 'a problem'. They gave no details and they did not mention that either of them had been married before. 'This was mainly because I was a bit doubtful about her,' admitted Joyce. 'I suspected that she might just feed back to us some fanciful variation of any information we supplied. . . . '

Soon the medium was talking intensely about jealousy. It was enshrouding Joyce, she said, and it was clouding her entire life. Then to their total surprise, she mentioned the name 'Bridget'. 'Bridget is here with you, she is an unsettled and very unhappy spirit.'

Howard then started talking about Bridget. He was completely frank about the miseries in that first marriage. He said a great deal which Joyce had not heard before and which gave her a deeper understanding of this 'phantom wife'. This was the right moment, she decided, for Howard also to be given a fuller insight into the truth. She had not had the courage before to describe the full extent of her private agony. She had never told him about how she had kept hearing the name 'Bridget'. There had been several times when she had been tempted to do so, because she had yearned for his reassurance and help, but she had been frightened that he might misunderstand. He might feel that she was being neurotic, that she was being stupidly jealous over a woman who was dead.

The medium addressed herself to Bridget's spirit: 'You have had your life on earth. Now you must let Howard and Joyce have their lives. You are to go away and be happy.' And she gave Joyce this advice: 'If you are troubled in that way again you should make this sign of the Cross and say – "Please give me the light of thy protection, Lord."'

Joyce used the prayer often during the following weeks. It soothed the tensions she felt fermenting inside her but it was obvious that she was still harbouring the spirit of Bridget. She and Howard decided to seek aid from an expert.

In July Joyce was exorcised by Father Wheaton at the Oratory of Our Lady in Exeter. I have kept in close contact with the Pettigrews since that ceremony. Their lives have changed completely. There is no sign of Bridget. And Joyce, once again, can sing.

* * *
* * *

The fact that Bridget Pettigrew had died unexpectedly in tragic circumstances must be regarded as potentially significant, for priests claim that possession by the human dead – or the creation of a baleful atmosphere by 'over-shadowing' – is often evidenced after a tragedy.

Father Ian Hazlewood describes having to clear such over-shadowing after a young man committed suicide. The man had married into a wealthy Gloucestershire family and his father-in-law had given the couple a farm as a wedding present. This gift was soon to have a disastrous consequence. The man worked hard on the farm and developed it into a profitable enterprise. Yet he could not rid himself of the thought that he owed the foundation of his success entirely to his father-in-law. That belief brought a feeling of inadequacy which gnawed at him and made him severely depressed. His wife tried to reassure him, so did his friends. It made no difference. He saw himself as a failure and started to despise himself. Eventually he shot himself.

Soon after the funeral his father-in-law had a disconcerting feeling that he was never entirely on his own. It was as if he constantly accompanied by an unseen presence – one which exuded great anguish. He suffered this sensation for months, hoping it would pass, before seeking the help of Father Hazlewood.

'This may sound strange and perhaps even a little crazy. . . ' he began apologetically. 'But my son-in-law is with me all the time. I can't explain how I know it's him but I *do* know. . . '

Father Hazlewood nodded understandingly. He and his helper, a lay Christian sensitive, were familiar with the oppressive symptoms of over-shadowing and, within a short while, he was satisfied that this man had made the correct diagnosis. He addressed himself to the spirit of the dead man – gave him absolution, invoked the protection of the angels and the prayers of the Blessed Virgin. Then he gave God's blessing and commanded the spirit to go in peace.

Father Hazlewood told me: 'His spirit was then released and his father-in-law, in that moment, was relieved of his burden.'

* * *
* * *

Horror can also follow the tragic death of a stranger. That was demonstrated by the frenzy of psychic violence, eventually witnessed by policemen, which devastated the home of the Burden family in Bournemouth.

More than two years of terrror started there early in 1979 when Bradley Burden, then aged six, was admiring new decorative candles which were on the sideboard. There were five of them and their designs attracted him. He stared at them in childish delight and, within seconds, each of them sprouted flames. There was no-one near them at the time and there were no matches in the room.

That was what his foster parents, Charles and Catherine Burden, told their neighbours. They did not believe them. Such a happening, they felt, was impossible. They were also sceptical a few weeks later when the Burdens described how their bed had mysteriously burst into flames. The fire had probably been started by a cigarette, they felt, or perhaps by an electric blanket. Neither of the Burdens smoke, nor was there an electric blanket on their bed. Mr Burden says that during the following years he and his wife – together with Bradley and their teenage daughter, Deborah – witnessed a range of curious but comparatively minor phenomena in their home.

The temperature in rooms would suddenly drop for no apparent reason and small objects moved of their own accord, usually when Bradley was near them.

'It was very upsetting, but apart from the time when we had the fire in our bed there didn't seem to be any danger. I didn't understand much then about ghosts or exorcisms or anything like that and I didn't realise there was anything that could be done.'

On Friday 14 August 1981, however, he was forced to call the police because of a mammoth eruption of inexplicable violence.

'And they didn't believe me either at first, they thought I must be some sort of crackpot.' That was hardly surprising. People with little experience of the occult might well have regarded his story with suspicion.

The house had seemed particularly chilly that morning when he had got up at five and their Labrador – which had reacted before to 'changes in the atmosphere' – would not stop howling. When Charles left for work at six the dog ran into the street and could not be coaxed back into the house. Two hours later Mrs Burden heard a crashing sound from the sitting-room. 'I went in to see what had happened and the table flew around the room. Then the biscuit tin whizzed past my head and crashed on the floor. Other objects started moving and tumbling around and I was petrified. It was a disaster area.'

Her first thought was that this havoc was being caused by the ghost of a man who had hanged himself six years earlier in a nearby house. Newspapers reported that theory but subsequent developments indicated that it was wrong. Bradley ran next door for help and Mrs Burden managed to contact her husband by telephone. He returned within half an hour: 'The place looked as if a tornado had been through it. There was debris scattered through the downstairs rooms and furniture had been knocked over. An oil heater in the hall fell over about the time I got there and another one slid across the floor in the kitchen. Plants were also tumbling and plates suddenly started flying around the kitchen. When I called the police it was as if the telephone was being snatched out of my hand. One minute I was holding it and then it was jerked away from me and was being thrown around like the plates.'

Sergeant Alan Wood and PC Graham Joyce arrived.

'By then things had quietened down and they wouldn't believe me – not even when they saw the damage,' said Mr Burden. 'They seemed to think that I'd probably been having a fight with my wife.'

Their doubts were soon dispelled, however, for they all watched aghast as a kitchen dresser toppled over to send still more plates and dishes crashing to the floor. PC Joyce reported, 'There was a tremendous crash and the dresser went over. It would normally have taken two men to shift it. It was very eerie and there was just no logical explanation. It was very cold inside compared with the heat of the blazing sun outside.'

The policemen advised them to call in a retired priest, ninety-five-year-old Dr Fred Oliver, to exorcise the house. Dr Oliver performed the service that day and said afterwards: 'There has been something of evil in this house that has fed on fear, but now it has gone.'

Chief Inspector Peter Williams of Bournemouth police commented: 'It is one of these weird unexplained incidents. The matter is now closed.'

On 15 August the *Daily Telegraph* headlined its report *Priest rids house of evil after police face poltergeist*. But by the time that newspaper was being read there was another 'psychic whirlwind'. The pervading coldness in the house, which had gone after the exorcism, returned and objects were once again being hurtled around.

Mr and Mrs Burden, advised by a social worker, evacuated the house with their children. This social worker also introduced them to two mediums who conducted a second exorcism on the Saturday morning. Their efforts, like those of Dr Oliver, brought temporary relief. It was as if the intrusive spirit was merely ducking away from them – lying low to give the impression it had gone. After their departure it again came out of hiding and gave yet another display of its fearsome power.

There was no possibility of the family being able to live in the house, which had been their home for ten years, but it seemed they could expect little help from the local authority. Bournemouth's housing manager, Basil Willcox said: 'We have the utmost sympathy for the family but they are not without shelter and cannot be treated as homeless. If the house were deemed physically unfit for human habitation then the local authority would have a statutory duty to rehouse. But I understand a poltergeist relates to a family and not to a house.'

But what is a poltergeist?

> The haunting characterised by noise and displacement is commonly called a poltergeist haunting . . . poltergeist

> phenomena at different times and different places show a curious parallelism. One feature that nearly all have in common is the presence of a young person, boy or girl, somewhere between the ages of twelve and twenty. This fact led many of the early observers to suppose that all poltergeist phenomena were products of normal mischief. Many cases, however, cannot be explained in this way without much straining of the evidence. There seems to be better ground for supposing that the phenomena (whether normal or paranormal) are products of mental strain in the young person concerned. (*Encyclopaedia Britannica 1963.*)

In this Bournemouth case, at first glance, it would seem that the problems were stemming from young Bradley. So at that stage there was justification for the attitude taken by the housing manager. Subsequent events suggested, however, that Bradley was merely being used as an unwitting source of energy – that an alien entity was draining him and operating through him. The bizarre happenings in the house were not 'poltergeist activity' in the sense that most people understand the phrase. They were caused by the earthbound spirit of a man who had died prematurely and tragically.

The mediums felt they were dealing with a singularly tenacious adversary and that, before making another attempt at exorcism, they needed reinforcements. Five of them held a seance that night in a darkened room at the house – hoping to make direct contact with the spirit and to help ease its journey to another sphere.

They sat in a circle, pooling their emotional and mental energies into a form of invitation to the spirit – reassuring it and willing it to make contact in order to be identified. Their leader was ready to become the 'instrument' – the person through whose voicebox the spirit could communicate. I have listened to spirit voices which have spoken in this way through Ted Riggs, one of the most highly regarded mediums and spiritualist healers in Britain, and I can confirm that they are too dissimilar to his voice for there to be any possibility of trickery. The voices I heard came from the mouth of Ted Riggs. But they were voices from beyond the grave. And it was another of those voices which the mediums were hoping to hear.

'My wife had had more than enough by then and was too frightened to go near the place,' said Mr Burden. 'I was very apprehensive as well but it was my home and I felt it was my duty to be there.'

He sat in at the seance and, after a short while, he heard the voice of the spirit.

'It was that of a man who told us quite a bit about himself. He was a drug addict who'd been living in Bournemouth and who'd died horribly because of his addiction.'

The man's death had occurred early in 1979 – shortly before the episodes with the candles and the burning bed.

'He said he wanted to join his grandmother, who'd died some years before, but he couldn't find the way,' said Mr Burden. 'He was angry and frustrated and he'd been working off his feelings through Bradley.'

Young children tend to be more receptive to psychic influences than adults. That was why Bradley was the most vulnerable member of this family. However, one of the principal attractions for the spirit of this dead man – according to information received during the seance – was Burden's teenage daughter.

Mr Burden told me, 'He kept saying disgusting and obscene things, things I couldn't bring myself to repeat, about his attitudes to Deborah. It was very obvious that he regarded her as sexually attractive. At the height of the seance his presence was very strong and the mediums said it would have been possible then to have made him appear in a physical form. They didn't want to do that because there'd be no benefit and so they switched on the lights to stop him appearing.'

Spiritualist mediums prefer to work in darkness or semi-darkness and this often provokes speculation about the credibility of their results. Many people suspect that light is avoided simply to make deception that much simpler. Spiritualists claim that physical manifestations can be achieved satisfactorily only if there is slowing down of the vibration rate of the ether. Light creates transverse waves through the ether and disrupts it to such an extent that a materialisation is virtually impossible. So bright lights destroy the essential atmosphere.

The mediums have claimed that, before the lights were turned on, they had introduced the dead drug addict to a spirit guide who would then be showing him his future path.

'He seemed very different by the end of the seance,' I was told. 'He seemed to be happy and relieved because he was at last going to be reunited with his grandmother.'

Two weeks later the family moved back into the house. There were no further manifestations. I checked again a month later. 'There are no longer any problems of that nature here. The man's spirit has gone.'

* * *
* * *

How long can a restless spirit remain earthbound and continue to intrude on the living? Claims that such hauntings can continue for generations would seem to be substantiated by the violence which took Father John Wheaton to an isolated seventeenth-century farmhouse in Devon. His help was sought there by a family – husband, wife, son and two daughters – soon after they had moved into the property.

It was the elder daughter who first became aware of a 'presence'. 'I was woken up at about three o'clock in the morning by what sounded like heavy breathing. It was very loud, as if someone or something was right next to my bed. I lay listening for a few minutes, to make sure I was really awake, and then I turned on the bedside light. The noise stopped immediately and there was nothing in the room. I read for a while, thinking that maybe I'd imagined it, and then it started again. Some invisible creature was in the room, very close to me, and breathing heavily.'

She fled along a corridor to her parents' room. The mystery breathing had stopped again by the time they went to investigate. But that night was only the beginning. Two weeks later the mother was awakened at three o'clock by a similar noise. 'It certainly wasn't coming from my husband, who was asleep beside me, but it was very near the bed. At first, my logic refused to accept what I was hearing but the sound was unmistakable. It was like the laboured breathing of someone who was probably overweight and middle-aged. And judging by the height it was coming from, I estimated that the person was more than six feet.' She turned on the light. The sound stopped immediately.

Her impression of the phantom's size seemed to be confirmed shortly afterwards by a family friend who spent a night there. She described seeing 'a big man with whiskers in an old-fashioned military uniform who appeared very briefly and then vanished'. The time, again, was around three o'clock.

At the same time on a different night another guest – a woman from Jersey visiting with her husband and fourteen-year-old son – was disturbed by 'something in the room'. I checked with this woman, who insists she had known nothing of the house's reputation, and she said she woke with a start, sure that someone was standing beside the bed. The impression was so vivid she thought it must be her son. She mentioned the incident at breakfast and was told about the ghost.

Events started to develop more ominously.

The younger daughter, aged ten, was awakened at about three by a weight on her stomach. 'It felt as if a man was sitting on me and I was very frightened. I screamed at him and he got off.' That was the beginning of the physical contact. A heavy picture was moved by some invisible force across this child's room. A few evenings later she and her sister, watching television in an upstairs room, saw a book floating through the air. The elder girl remarked, 'It was as if someone had picked it up and had carried it about five yards before flinging it to the carpet.'

The younger girl became too frightened to be upstairs alone. Her bed was moved into her parents' room. 'And then I got a good thumping in my stomach, as if the thing had followed her in,' said the mother. 'We hadn't really minded the ghost being here when it was only doing heavy breathing, not after we'd got over our first feelings of alarm, but this repeated violence was very worrying. My husband and I realised it might start getting even more violent, perhaps with frustration over not being able to convey some message, and it might do serious harm to the children. We started to consider asking for an exorcism. . . '

They finally made the decision after a singularly startling attack on the elder girl. 'My sister had moved back into her own room and I was sleeping there with her. At about the usual time in the morning she started shouting that it was sitting on her again. There was an odd high-pitched sound in the room. I sat up in bed and shouted at the ghost to go away and leave her alone. And almost immediately I was slapped very hard across the face, as if the thing was furious with me for daring to interfere.'

Father Wheaton's ceremony of exorcism lasted for two hours. 'We were dealing with the spirit of a human being who had almost certainly been dead a hundred years or more and, through the power of Our Lord, I severed the chains which were keeping it a captive in the house. This was one of those exorcisms, unlike those involving elementals or demons, which was of benefit to the dead as well as the living.

'The regular time-pattern of the manifestations was linked with some great trauma experienced by the man – very likely his own physical death. An earth-bound spirit can remain undetected in a house for many years, as if in a state of hibernation, until there are suitable people for it to draw energy from and become active. That's clearly what happened here.'

I monitored the situation at that house for more than a year after the exorcism. There was no repetition of the haunting. The father commented, 'There's been another big difference since Father Wheaton's visit. Rooms which always had the edge of chilliness are warmer and the whole atmosphere seems far happier.'

6 The distinctive smell of evil

Exorcism is often considered necessary in homes where there have been no sightings of ghosts and no violent phenomena, homes where the reported troubles seem more intangible and less easy to define. One of the first exorcisms I attended was performed to banish the source of a singularly unpleasant smell. That may strike some people as unlikely because bad smells are traced more often to faulty drains than to lurking spirits. It is firmly believed, however, that certain alien entities can be identified by their distinctive odours.

This 'smell' exorcism was conducted by Father Wheaton at the home of a surveyor and his wife, near the Imperial War Museum in south London. It is a gaunt three-storied building with grey and yellow brickwork grimed by a century of soot and dirt.

Later I was able to establish a fact not known at the time to Father Wheaton or the owners – that many years earlier this house had been the scene of a brutal murder.

There are now spare bedrooms in the house's basement, which was once rented as a separate flat, and the smell was most obvious near the bottom of the thirteen narrow stairs leading to this area. It was first noticed by the surveyor's wife soon after they'd bought the property. 'It was peculiar and disgusting, like fish that had gone off. It came and went. At times it seemed to be following me from room to room as if, in some strange way, it was attached to me. Guests and other members of the family would become aware of it as soon as I walked in through a door. Then it would suddenly seem to have been switched off. It would simply go without any after-trace. Then, later, it would be back.

'My husband understands most of the things that can go

wrong in a house, because he's had years of experience as a surveyor, but he couldn't find any reason for the smell. It went on like this for about eighteen months – coming more often and getting stronger and stronger – until, in the end, I hated being here. I don't consider that I'm psychic in any way, and I'd never experienced anything of a psychic nature before, but I had a terrible feeling that there was something basically wrong about the place. The atmosphere seemed uneasy, even when there wasn't the smell, and I reached the pitch where I was frightened of being here on my own.'

Friends stayed with her when her husband was away on business. One was a medium who told her that the house was being plagued by an elemental and that the smell would keep recurring unless the building were cleansed by exorcism.

One Sunday afternoon, a couple of weeks later, Father Wheaton went to the house to perform an exorcism. A bookcase served as a makeshift altar in a corridor near the front door. On it he placed a silver cross, flanked by candles, and a bowl of holy water. We stood before it for a brief service of prayer. Then he went from room to room with the holy water and a censer in which frankincense and cinnamon were smouldering on wafers of charcoal. Every cupboard was opened to receive the incense and a sprinkling of the water so that no niche was left uncleansed. Everywhere throughout the building he repeated the command: 'In the name of God which is above every other name, I exorcise all influences of evil. . . '

He then repeated the entire process. Neither Father Wheaton nor I was conscious of any presence of evil. 'But that's not particularly significant because I don't consider that either of us is particularly sensitive and, anyway, as I've said before, elementals are not really evil. What they often do is to latch on to a human being who is emitting the right sort of energy – tapping that energy in order to become more powerful – and this is probably why the smell was sometimes almost a part of the woman,' he said.

Now we could only hope that this elemental – if, indeed, the problems had been caused by one – had gone to its appointed sphere.

There was still one precaution to be taken. The house has to be blessed and all entrances sealed, with the love of God, to prevent any 'further intrusion by unwanted spirits'.

Father Wheaton went outside and, as he re-entered, said formally: 'Peace be to this house and to all that dwell herein.' He drew a line with holy water across the base of the front doorway. 'We pray Thee, O Lord, so to bless this doorway by Thy mighty power that those who enter here may leave behind them all unworthy thought and feeling and that Thy children who dwell in this place may ever serve Thee in peace and holiness of life. Through Christ our Lord, Amen.'

He repeated this prayer at all the other entrances and then concluded: 'O God, who in Thy providence has appointed a wondrous ministry of angels, we pray Thee to send down Thy holy angel to bless and hallow this house. . . '

Through the following months there was no longer any hint of the smell. The presumed elemental had gone. The woman's fear of being alone at night finally lifted.

By then I had completed my researches into the history of the house. During the early stages of World War II it had been unoccupied and was vandalised. Drunks and vagrants used it as a doss-house. In 1941 one of these vagrants, a middle-aged man, was found at the foot of the stairs to the basement. He had been repeatedly stabbed in the stomach and chest.

Could there have been a direct forty-year link between the apparent infestation and the murder?

'We could never be definite on the point but it would be a logical assumption,' said Father Wheaton. 'When blood is shed there is an instant release of energy which can affect the spiritual atmosphere. This was understood by the ancients and was the basis for blood sacrifices.

'This energy can attract elementals which can draw strength from it and use it to become manifest. But it's also possible, of course, that this spirit was in the house for many years before the murder – having been helped to develop, perhaps, through some earlier act of violence. All we can say for certain is that it was there and that it was cast out through the power of Our Lord.'

A foul smell was also a key factor in the ordeal of another family, recalled by Prebendary Egerton Walters who now lives near Brecon.

When he was a parish priest at Shrewsbury in 1966 he was called in by a frightened family living in a rambling, 200-year-old house only 200 yards from his vicarage. Electric wiring had been ripped out in the middle of the night. Wardrobes had been overturned and clothing scattered. A Bible in a bedroom had been torn to pieces. The family's Alsatian refused to stay in the house at night and the husband reported, 'Most nights we see a dark shape which gives off a smell so repulsive that it is unbelievable.' This pattern of haunting persisted for a month.

Prebendary Walters spent a great deal of time in the house, questioning and checking, before requesting help from his Bishop, who 'seemed rather sceptical'.

The Bishop did agree to bless the house, although he later denied having performed an exorcism, and after his visit there were no further disturbances. Prebendary Walters has confirmed these details to me in writing: 'If the Bishop did not actually exorcise the house, he did come very near to it by the prayers and the blessing which he gave. The family had cause to be very distressed by their experiences and were very relieved when they ceased after the Bishop's visit. I felt that there was no doubt that some evil influence had been removed by the power of the Holy Spirit.'

* * *
* * *

Many exorcists regard smell as a diagnostic aid when they are considering the possibility of individuals being possessed. They say it helps confirm the presence of an alien spirit.

After Father Hazlewood had met the demoniac at his vicarage in Gloucestershire he reported that 'there was an unpleasant smell coming from him'. Evangelist Jimmy Gemmell of Carlisle claims that a distinctive 'rancid stink' often accompanies psychic evil. He calls it demon odour.

There could be a far more mundane explanation for such a

'stink', of course, because many of the people seeking help are in an appalling mental state and, as a result, tend to be careless about personal hygiene. The smell could be caused by lack of soap and water, rather than by a possessing demon, and would then be nothing more than body odour.

However, exorcists insist that they treat such a smell in a careful perspective – regarding it only as an additional symptom which points to the core of the problem.

Mr Gemmell describes being sickenly aware of 'demon odour' shortly after three o'clock in the morning when his wife, Jean, was awakened by the telephone. The caller was distraught and near to hysterics. Her daughter, she explained between sobs, was in a 'terrible state'. Could Mr Gemmell come immediately?

'Wouldn't it be a good idea for you to call your doctor?' suggested Mr Gemmell.

'No!' The reply was vehement. This was not a matter for any doctor. The only person who'd know what to do was Mr Gemmell. And, please, could he come right away . . .

The daughter had suffered a broken marriage, had a history of alcoholism and occasionally worked as a prostitute. The Gemmells drove to a flat near Carlisle where, in the livingroom, they saw why the older woman had been so desperate. The daughter, partially dressed, was 'writhing on the floor like a serpent'.

She hissed loudly at Mr Gemmell as if in warning and, when he moved towards her, she squirmed under a table in an attempt to hide. She had not been taking drink or drugs, according to her mother, who added that there had been earlier attacks. Not one of them, however, had been so acute.

Mr Gemmell told me: 'She had been putting herself at risk by selling herself to so many men. There's a great awareness of how diseases can be contracted through sexual intercourse but few people realise that intercourse can also bring spiritual pollution. This is another of the reasons for the continual increase in the need for exorcism. Society's permissive attitudes have created an atmosphere in which vast numbers of youngsters – and, indeed, people who are not so young – regard bed-hopping as perfectly normal behaviour. I am not simply preaching morality here, although I do have strong feelings on that subject, for it is essential to stress the unseen spiritual risks. Physical contact can help the transmission of power for good or evil – as we can see with the healers who lay on hands – and this woman almost certainly been entered by a man who was demon-infected.'

This dread of contamination by physical contact is one shared by officially-appointed exorcists in the Church of England. Some say they would never lay hands on a person believed to be possessed by a demon because they feel there is a danger of an alien spirit crossing that bridge of flesh.

This conjures up a faintly ludicrous idea of a tiny but determined thing, a sort of invisible multi-legged microbe, seizing the opportunity to scuttle into new territory. The concept seems to offer a gross over-simplification of what is regarded as spiritual evil. Even a flea can hop from one host to another and germs can float through the air. It is peculiar that demons – credited with such astonishing powers – should be considered less versatile in their mobility. However, that is the view held by many exorcists.

Mr Gemmell believed that this woman had probably been to bed with 'a man who was demon-infected'. His initial suspicion that she was possessed was confirmed when he got closer to her and identified demon odour.

She was still writhing and hissing defiance as he started the exorcism: 'In the name of Jesus Christ, I come against you Satan and demon powers; I bind you in the Almighty Name . . .'

Suddenly she got up – no longer a snake but a hate-filled harridan. She started screaming, blaspheming and threatening.

At such times Mr Gemmell mentally recalls the words addressed to the Ephesians by St Paul: 'Put on the full armour of God so that you can take your stand against the devil's schemes . . . so that when the day of evil comes, you may be able to stand your ground . . . take up the shield of faith with which you can extinguish all the flaming arrows of the evil one . . .'

Mr Gemmell was confident that he had the 'full armour' and the 'shield of faith'. And, while the demoniac was abusing him and trying to strike him, he continued resolutely with the exorcism. Suddenly she was quiet and still. She sat on a chair, with her arms folded across her chest, and started rocking backwards and forwards. 'The demon was still in her but it could no longer do harm for it was bound by the power of the Lord. I decided it was safe to leave it there and cast it out completely later that day.'

The mother agreed that the Gemmells should take the young woman back to their home. They were due to set off that morning on an evangelical crusade through central Scotland and it was there, in a Baptist Church, that Mr Gemmell completed the exorcism.

The woman was withdrawn but well-behaved and compliant, up to the moment when she was kneeling in the church. But then she began to 'howl like a dog' and vomitted. That was the moment the demon departed. But this was merely the start of the recovery. For the next six months she continued to live with the Gemmells. They supervised her behaviour, 'to make certain she didn't expose herself again to contamination', and they prayed with her daily. Eventually, she was rehabilitated to a normal life.

* * *
* * *

Apparitions which have no smell are reported in their hundreds and most of them can best be described as 'phoney phantoms'. Observers may genuinely see the figures of people who are long since dead but researchers believe that few of these sights indicate a spiritual presence. A vast number of the 'acknowledged hauntings' are not hauntings at all but the product of a phenomenon called the 'memory imprint'.

A typical example is occasionally witnessed at Kay Booth's 300-year-old cottage at Colyton, Devon. Near the front of the cottage, just along the lane, is a funeral parlour with a chapel of rest. The neat walled garden, with its shrubbery and sweep of patio, used to be a slaughter yard. Behind is the parish church with its rows of ancient graves. Many believe the cottage is haunted. These are people who, like Mrs Booth, have seen the 'grey lady' scuttling across the garden towards the front door.

They are convinced that this is the spirit of a woman who lived in the cottage a hundred years or so ago. They are wrong. There is no such spirit here. The lady in grey is certainly dead and is probably buried in the near-by churchyard. It is also highly likely that she once lived in the cottage or that she was a regular visitor. However, she is not a ghost but merely a memory imprint. It is rather as if a video tape of long-ago action was being played, time and time again, on the etheric screen.

The etheric screen has intrigued and baffled generations of scientists. The *Encyclopaedia Britannica* (1963) gives the following definition:

> A hypothetical substance filling all space, inclusive of those volumes occupied by ordinary matter and serving to transmit those forces (gravitational, electric, magnetic) which one material object exerts on another located at a distance . . . During the nineteenth century the ether hypothesis was accepted by all competent authorities, although there was a diversity of opinion as to the ether's properties. After 1900 the opposite opinion gained ground; namely that the hypothesis is unnecessary for the explanation of any observed phenomena. A few physicists still hold to the older view that an ether must exist and that otherwise philosophical difficulties would arise in connection with the concept of action-at-a-distance . . . traditionally, space has been conceived as an unchangeable, passive constituent of the universe, neither affecting nor being affected by the dynamic changes occurring in the material parts of the universe. On this view, space is analogous to the moving-picture screen which remains unaltered even when the most violent scenes are projected upon it, and neither aids nor hinders the action, though its presence is necessary for the perception of the pictures.

Father Arnold Clare has described ether, rather more graphically as being like a 'motionless invisible jelly' which fills all the space around us and within us. It is an isotropic substance in that it has constant properties, particularly with respect to elasticity or to refraction for rays of the same wavelength. Air and light can pass freely through it and, in the right circumstances, it can absorb and retain kinetic energy – a fact which is said to explain the sightings of memory imprints. Energy radiated by certain people, possibly at times of intense emotion, has been captured in this 'jelly' and, when conditions are suitable, it can be seen as a form of 'action replay'.

There is also a theory that the pull of gravity is strengthened by the weight of the ether. Sir Isaac Newton considered this a strong possibility but did not publish his views because he 'was not able from experiment and observation to give a satisfactory account of this medium, and the manner of its operation in producing the chief phenomena of nature' *(Encyclopaedia Britannica,* 1889).

The problems which confounded Newton and later investigators – such as Michael Faraday, who was regarded as the founder of electrochemistry – arose because all experiments are conducted within the etheric mass. Even the 'empty expanses of space', it is said, are filled with ether. So it is not possible to get outside it in order to weigh it, for example, and the situation is complicated still further by the assertion that ether also permeates our bodies. This, if true, puts us in the position of a living sponge in the depths of the ocean. It is so accustomed to being filled with water and surrounded by water that it could never recognise that there is such a substance as water.

Modern physicists are still trying to resolve the mystery of the ether. When they do succeed many of today's 'paranormal phenomena' will be explained by science. There will then be a more easily appreciated rationalisation of occurrences such as sightings of memory imprints.

Kay Booth told me, 'I saw her for the first time in 1972 after I'd had a section of wall replaced by a window. I wasn't expecting a caller and I thought that perhaps she was someone collecting for charity. By the time I'd opened the front door, however, she'd gone. The garden was empty and the gate was still locked.'

Imprint apparitions are often sighted after alterations to buildings. They are then more likely to be seen because, it is claimed, they are agitated over changes in places with which they have a strong link. This implies that these shadow images can experience anxiety or anger, that they are capable of feeling possessive. The truth is far simpler: structural changes often bring them more easily into view. This was demonstrated at a house near Henley in the Thames Valley where a games-room extension was built in the garden. The owner was astonished to see a stag pursued by hounds and a monk on horseback charge through the wall and the billiard table. This phantom chase had probably been taking place regularly for many years, unseen in the darkness of the garden, and now it was merely continuing to follow its original course. The grey lady, similarly, had almost certainly been hurrying across the garden for generations. But she had not been seen until the window was installed in 1972.

'I'm so used to her now that I no longer bother to go to the door. But visitors often tell me that there's a woman crossing the garden . . .'

There is a serene atmosphere in Mrs Booth's home and she certainly has no worries about her spectre. 'In fact, I'd miss her if she stopped coming. I regard her almost as a friend.'

The overwhelming majority of apparitions described as ghosts – at least eighty per cent and probably more – are memory imprints which can linger for hundreds of years. The clothing of some seen recently by credible witnesses suggest that they are images of people who died in the sixteenth century or even earlier.

Imprints are often seen in churches, prisons and hospitals. Two imprints of monks have been reported in Westminster Abbey and one of a middle-aged man in a gallery at Exeter Prison. A 'phantom small girl' is said to have been observed on a number of occasions at London's Central Middlesex Hospital.

I do not doubt that such visions are often seen but I challenge the explanation offered by many psychic researchers. There is a tendency to link automatically the apparitions with violent and sudden deaths – to regard them as spirits which, not accepting the reality of their physical deaths, are unable to find rest.

Professional ghost-hunters are quick to point out that two monks were murdered during the fourteenth century in Westminster Abbey. At Exeter Prison they see a similar convenient pattern. The 'phantom' was seen near the spot once used for executions. And the small girl at the Central Middlesex Hospital is identified as the ghost of a child who died during an operation in the 1970s.

All very neat and logical. But is it true?

Energy generated by terror or desperation, during brutal or premature deaths, certainly could scorch imprints on the etheric screen. But this argument is offered too often and too glibly. Many investigators treat tragedy almost as an essential – primarily because it 'spices' an alleged haunting – and their conclusions can create confusion.

Consider the many passionately religious men who, through the centuries, have been a part of the daily life in Westminster Abbey. Some have radiated exceptional vitality and, while alive, would have made deep impressions on those around them and on the atmosphere. Could it not be that subsequent sightings are a legacy of those impressions? The fact that there were two murdered monks, whose personalities may have been far less vibrant, does not necessarily have any significance.

Many baleful and fanciful stories have been weaved around imprint apparitions. Some are said to be harbingers of doom and their appearance is regarded as a warning of impending death. This is nonsense. However, there are circumstances in which imprints can bring dangers.

Motorists are continually claiming to have seen phantoms which may take the form of people, dogs, vintage cars or even stage-coaches carrying passengers from another century. They have swerved to avoid them, because they look so startingly solid, and have then realised that they have vanished. How many of these swerves have produced serious accidents? How many have ended in death?

Baffled survivors have often protested: 'He must have been crazy. He pulled over without warning – right in front of me.' They could not start to understand that the 'crazy' driver might have been reacting normally and instinctively – trying to avoid hitting the imprint of a person who, very possibly, had been buried for many years.

Imprints cannot be exorcised in the usual sense of the word

and most of them should be regarded merely as harmless and rather intriguing quirks of cosmology. Efforts can be made, however, to erase those causing danger or genuine distress. This was explained to me by the Reverend Dr Donald Omand, who has an impressive international reputation as an exorcist. Dr Omand, the son of a Church of Scotland minister, was initially ordained as a Free Church minister in 1937. In 1954 he was ordained into the Church of England at Christ Church, Oxford, and most of his service in the Church, until his retirement, was spent as vicar of Chideock, Devon. He has been called upon to perform exorcisms in most parts of Britain, often accompanied by Terry Glanville, a medical doctor, who acts as a witness. He has also worked in fifteen other countries. Many of the problems he has investigated have been caused by imprints. He reported, 'In these circumstances, prayer is the only effective answer. The priest must be one who has a keen understanding of the problem. God will listen to his prayers, because they are carefully considered and completely unselfish, and He will then, as it were, wipe the blackboard clean.'

Dr Omand knows. There have been several occasions when he has used such prayers; at a road black-spot between Charmouth and Morcambelake in Dorset where seventeen accidents had been reported in six months. Subsequently they ceased altogether.

Jimmy Gemmell claims to have had similar success on a main road north of Carlisle. 'For years there'd been a terrible spate of accidents and near-accidents and drivers kept telling police the same story: they had swerved to avoid two people who had suddenly appeared in the road. One motorist was sure that he must have hit them. Yet there hadn't been any bump and, when he went back to investigate, the road was completely empty.'

The spectral jaywalkers were not reported again, he says, after he prayed for them to be removed in the name of Jesus.

7 Controversy in the medical profession

Should the medical profession be making more use of exorcism? Should the rituals be considered to have possible benefits for patients with mental disorders?

These questions have inspired heated debates between psychiatrists. Many use exorcism regularly, in partnership with priests, as an alternative form of treatment. Many others regard it as superstitious idiocy which can exacerbate medical problems.

Dr Sandy Robertson, a consultant psychiatrist at Kidderminster General Hospital, has attacked the work of a local evangelical exorcist: 'I baulk at the idea that there is a disembodied entity which can enter people. For most people ideas such as possession and witchcraft are obvious nonsense but for some suggestible people they seem to provide a ready explanation for conflicts and turmoil which really arise within themselves. These ideas can only add an element of superstitious fear to an already troubled mind.'

This matches the view expressed to me by Professor Sir William Trethowan, head of the Department of Psychiatry at the University of Birmingham, who launched an attack on exorcism in *The Journal of Medical Ethics* in 1976:

> While many might insist that the time is long past for such nonsense, at least in a seemingly civilised society such as we might like to believe our own to be, the matter still crops up, occasionally with disastrous consequences . . .
>
> From time to time doctors encounter patients who suffer from delusions of possession which are symptomatic of an ongoing psychotic illness. These do not, as a general rule,

give rise to undue concern, for the fact that the subjects are mentally ill is usually fairly readily discernible, so that they are soon given appropriate treatment.

More problematic, possibly, are other not necessarily psychotic but severely neurotic patients who exhibit hysterical and other symptoms and behaviour which resembles that occurring in so-called possession states, both in medieval and more modern times. If such symptoms and behaviour are not recognised for what they really are, ie, due to mental abnormality, the sufferers may not only fall into wrong hands but be subjected to inappropriate treatment, including exorcism. The misguided application of such procedures may amount to frank mismanagement and can have dire results . . .

It is clear that man's idea of the existence of the devil almost certainly springs from his need to repudiate his deep-seated instinctual drives such as are concerned with lust, hate, envy and aggression and which, by their very nature, are so likely to arouse in him feelings of guilt. Following Freud, it would seem also that the most common way in which man divorces himself from his own sense of vileness is via the psychological mechanism of projection. Strength is lent to this defence mechanism by a fantasy of evil as something personified. Thus is the devil brought to life while at the same time man is at least partly relieved of the responsibility for some of his more bestial actions. In this way the tale as told all too readily becomes 'It was not I, but the devil who made me do it'.

Just as . . . an absolute belief in demoniacal possession creates a need for an exorcist, so, in turn, does a belief in the effects of exorcism create a need to believe in the devil. How else can an exorcist possibly justify his existence?

But is it really that simple? Not in the view of the *Yorkshire Post* which explored the question of exorcism being considered as a treatment for violent mental patients. In August 1980 the paper gave this editorial opinion:

The proposal is not as way-out as some people might imagine.

With proper safeguards, under strict professional supervision, and when orthodox methods appear to be failing, exorcism might well produce miracles in a great number of such cases.

In fact, there is an abundance of evidence to suggest that exorcism can work, and many psychiatrists and others who accept such evidence would describe themselves as agnostics or even atheists. It hardly matters, in the clinical and health context, what the mechanics are. In those cases where exorcism appears to work without disastrous side-effects, the argument between the religionists and the behaviourists is purely academic. Even atheists would think it a sin to let someone continue to suffer the agony of serious mental disturbance rather than let a priest administer a cure.

What the patient believes is probably more important than what the priest or the doctor believes. But if what cynics would call mumbo-jumbo does more practical good than insulin, the families of the afflicted would be the last people to carp . . .

The proposal for this possible recognition of exorcism in hospitals had then just been submitted for consideration by the Minister of Health. And behind it was an extraordinary story which had started on a pitch black night in February 1965 when three Danish *au pair* girls were thumbing a lift near a wood in Surrey. A driver in his early thirties stopped and agreed to take them the short distance to Kingston upon Thames. They did not recognise him as a man who had appeared on television, a man whose pioneering social work had earned him the public acclaim of such people as Lord Longford and Lord Montgomery.

For years he had been leading two astonishingly contrasting lives. By day he was respected as an efficient business executive who, because of his strong streak of compassion, was the founder and joint chairman of a national organisation designed to help discharged prisoners. By night he felt goaded by 'invisible spirits' into acts of destruction and mindless violence – such as sniping with a high-powered rifle at house windows and at cars on motorways.

That man is Peter Thompson, now chairman of a mental-health reform group called the Matthew Trust which is still pressing the government to accept exorcism officially as a possible cure for some of the most dangerous patients in Britain. It is a form of treatment, he told me, which eventually helped resolve his own mental problems.

His attack on the hitch-hikers was the culmination of years of bizarre behaviour during which, on more than one occasion, he had tried to take his own life. He took a side turning into the wood that evening and switched off the engine. Then he picked up a knife from the carpet by his feet and, in the struggle which followed, two of the girls were injured.

The Old Bailey judge later made this intriguing comment: 'There are other people who should bear responsibility for what has happened.' He then passed sentence on Mr Thompson: 'You will be detained in Broadmoor under Section 60 of the Mental Health Act of 1959; the period of your detention to be decided by other authorities.'

There was a clash of opinion between those 'other authorities' four and a half years later when Mr Thompson was hoping to be discharged. His application was vigorously opposed by Broadmoor doctors but they were over-ruled by psychiatrists on the Mental Health Review Tribunal. He was released but deep inside he knew his stability was still precarious. He became so worried, in fact, that he applied, unsuccessfully, to be allowed back into Broadmoor.

'I was bedevilled by depressions. They were plaguing my life and I couldn't get rid of them. I went to one psychiatrist after another but they couldn't find the cause and there seemed to be no solution.'

Dr Ted Gurney, a medical missionary friend, suggested he should visit the South London 'surgery' of Ken Lock and the Reverend Michael Smith, who specialised in divine healing and in the Ministry of Deliverance.

'They laid hands on me and prayed over me in what sounded like a foreign language,' he said. 'I realise now that this was a heavenly language in which they were asking that the demon inside me should be expelled by the power of God.' There was no instant miracle. Or, rather, there was no immediate sign of any change. His moods were still black and his mind was in turmoil. However, a parallel can be drawn here with the curing of certain physical ailments. A patient does not necessarily feel any improvement, for instance the moment a virus is killed. Its debilitating impact lingers for a while in his system. He has had the appropriate treatment and it has been effective but he still needs time to 'get better'.

'It was nearly a week later when I suddenly realised that I had recovered completely,' said Peter Thompson. 'It was as if a heavy rucksack had been taken off my back. The depressions which had puzzled the psychiatrists had simply gone and, for the first time in years, I felt that my mind was clear.'

This experience, coupled with his own observations inside Broadmoor and his subsequent researches, convinced him that exorcism should be endorsed by the Department of Health. The Matthew Trust's report to the Health Minister claimed that this form of treatment could prove invaluable to certain patients in Britain's four special hospitals – Broadmoor, Rampton, Park Lane and Moss-Side. They accommodate about 2,300 patients and the average length of stay is between seven and ten years. Nearly ten per cent, however, are regarded as incurable and dangerous. They face the prospect of being kept in for life.

Mr Thompson recommends that for these patients in particular the authorities should offer carefully supervised services of exorcism. He said: 'There is no hope for them otherwise because they are considered undiagnosable. They are merely given tranquillisers to keep them stable. Most of them are people who have committed out-of-character crimes while mentally ill – or possibly while possessed by demons – but, because they cannot be diagnosed, the trigger that set them off hasn't been discovered. So they have to stay inside until the trigger is found. That means many of them stay inside for ever.

'All the traditional treatments have failed with these patients. That is why we want the Department of Health – in consultation with the British Medical Association, the appropriate unions and the established churches – to regard exorcism as an optional treatment which could be given only with the consent of a patient or with that of his guardians or relatives. That would at least give these patients some sort of chance.'

We were chatting over coffee in his Chelsea flat and it was difficult to credit that this well-groomed and articulate but gentle man – at one time a housemaster at a Barnardo's Children's Village – had once been too dangerous to be allowed his freedom.

He continued: 'Maybe it would be regarded as experimental but why should that be an objection? Experimental methods have been used in the past and are still being used. Over the years, for example, a lot of patients who have committed sexual offences have been tried with raw drugs – drugs which haven't been tested – and so those patients really were guinea-pigs. Many of them, particularly men, have been given electrical tests linked with their genitals. They have been told there is no other hope for them and so they may as well agree to have this treatment. The sinister thing about some of the experimental treatments is that the side-effects cannot be predicted. I know one patient, for instance, who developed breasts after having drug treatment for sexual problems. This is not unusual with certain drugs but he developed breasts such as you would expect to see on a large woman. That sort of side-effect, which can make a patient feel degraded and frightened and more disturbed than ever, could never happen with exorcism.

'We do not suggest that exorcism should be used indiscriminately. We recognise that if improperly administered it could lead to the patient becoming worse. We are merely asking the Health Minister to consider its use with patients who do not respond to normal treatments.

'In Broadmoor and the other special hospitals, there could be the great advantage of such services being conducted in a controlled situation – with psychiatrists, nurses and clergy working as a team. They would have all the facilities and monitoring devices to see that the patient was not being adversely affected. They would have access to drugs which might be needed to tranquillise the patient. All we are asking is that this should be given a trial by the Department of Health.'

What response has there been from the Department?

'The Minister replied that the treatment of patients should be left to individual psychiatrists. That really is absolute nonsense. Too many psychiatrists are so hidebound that they would automatically dismiss the idea of exorcism. They don't understand it, they don't believe in it, and they don't want to know about it. Some also resent the implication that a clergyman, without any medical qualifications, might be able to help where they have failed.'

During his years in Broadmoor did he meet any patients who, in his view, were victims of possession rather than of a diagnosable medical illness?

'Yes – five or six out of a patient population of about 700. But my judgement then would be in question because I was far from normal myself, of course, and I can make this evaluation only in retrospect.'

Had he later encountered any mental-hospital patients who had been possessed?

He replied without hesitation. 'Certainly. Only a few weeks ago, for instance, I was with an eighteen-year-old girl who had just been discharged after spending three years in a mental hospital. She had become seriously deranged at the age of fifteen and her parents had been told that she'd probably have to be kept inside for the rest of her life. There was no improvement in her condition and there seemed to be no prospect of any improvement. Then a visiting preacher, an evangelist, got her to accept Christ into her life – something she have never done before – and through him the demonic influences were exorcised. Six weeks later she was able to leave the hospital and start learning how to lead a normal life.'

Does he believe that eventually there will be a change in the government's attitude?

'We are attracting considerable support for such a change and we have the backing of some Members of Parliament but the whole subject is very touchy,' he said. 'The Department of Health would have a very rough time if it were to set up a joint consultative committee because exorcism is considered freakish. All the odd cases that have gone wrong would be dragged up and it would be a field-day for the media pundits. They would hammer the DHSS because we are now very much in a pagan society.'

This prospect of being 'hammered' or of being regarded as cranks is today inhibiting many people in the medical profession from allowing their views to be publicised. I have discussed the subject with psychiatrists who work on a regular basis with ordained exorcists – and with family doctors who discreetly arrange exorcisms in their surgeries – and nearly all of them have asked to remain anonymous. They believe they are achieving useful results but they are frightened of public opinion.

One of those with the courage to speak out is Dr Richard Mackarness, a psychiatrist in Hampshire, who told me: 'I am certain that there are unseen good and evil forces, that people can become possessed, and that sometimes the only effective treatment is exorcism.' He has had six patients whom he diagnosed as being possessed by demons and all of them were helped to recovery through Christian exorcism. Cases of possession are now becoming more frequent because of the 'explosion of interest in the occult'. He added: 'Every family doctor and psychiatrist should be on the alert for them because they can cause great distress. They can also end in suicide.'

He expanded his views in an article published in *The Practitioner* in 1974:

> The presenting psychiatric syndrome may be of any type, but more often than not a depressive, schizophrenic or schizo-affective label is attached by the psychiatrist first consulted. Appropriate treatment is given with little or no improvement, and the case is then often thrown open to discussion at a case conference as one of peculiar difficulty, and suggestions are invited from other psychiatrists.
>
> Invariably, when the true diagnosis turns out to be demonosis, a clear history of dabbling with the occult is obtained, usually just before the onset of the illness.
>
> It is not always the patient who has been directly involved with the spiritualism, ouija-board or black magic. Sometimes it is another member of the household.

He is referring here to the theory of contamination by

spill-over which I mentioned earlier. And he says that one of his patients, a 39-year-old woman, became possessed in this way. She had sought the aid of an amateur healer in the hope of ending her addiction to Valium – a drug which had been prescribed for her ten years earlier for a mild depressive illness.

Almost immediately afterwards she became highly disturbed, complaining that she had an 'unpleasant hot sensation' in her head and that she could hear 'horrible gasping-grunting noises'. Soon she was claiming that she could see the healer in her own home and hear him making suggestions of a sexual nature. She was taken into hospital where she was alarmed by 'black footprints' on the floor which could not be seen by anyone else.

Dr Mackarness reported: 'Weeks later we learned that this healer had admitted having used black magic.'

By then the woman had been diagnosed as a demoniac. The diagnosis was confirmed by Dr Kenneth McAll, a man with long experience as a surgeon and as a consultant psychiatrist, who is regarded as an authority on demonosis. He agreed that the patient should be exorcised.

Dr Mackarness wrote: 'I brought a crucifix from home and he did it in my office at the hospital, in my presence and with a nurse he brought with him to act as chaperone. The result was dramatic. The patient said she felt better at once and thereafter made an uninterrupted recovery.'

Dr McAll later questioned the healer and confirmed that 'he had been invoking black magic'.

Lay healers are often regarded with suspicion. Some are charlatans who prey on the desperate. However, there are those who achieve results which are truly remarkable. My investigations into their work have included interviews with many former patients – mostly people who had once been 'written-off' by the medical profession – who were still completely fit years after receiving healing.

I have cross-checked with some of the doctors concerned who, in case after case, have admitted to being baffled. One specialist, who had been unsuccessfully treating a young woman with a crippling and progressive spinal condition, chronic ankylosing spondylitis, told me: 'Her recovery, in medical terms, was quite impossible. Yet it happened. I can't offer any explanation.'

These facts need to be emphasised for any blanket denunciation of lay healers would be completely unjustified. The ordeal of Dr Mackarness's patient stemmed from the nature of this healer.

Two further cases were reported by Dr Mackarness: 'I referred for exorcism a woman with chronic alcoholism and had her cured after years of heavy, self-destructive drinking. Her drinking got out of hand when her mother-in-law, a malignant woman who dabbled in witchcraft, put a curse on her.

'Another patient, a young man who had started taking LSD at the instigation of a girlfriend who claimed to be a witch, developed what looked like a full-blown schizophrenic psychosis. He did very badly in hospital in spite of every known treatment for schizophrenia. In his case the demon took the form, in his mind, of a well-known Negro jazz musician who the patient looked upon with a mixture of fear and fascination and who he could hear and sometimes see around the ward. I tried to get it out of his system by persuading him to do a bust of this musician in our art department, but with no good effect. If anything, it made him worse. Eventually, the boy's father, a well-read man, suggested to me that his son was possessed by a devil. I agreed with him and referred the boy to Dr McAll for exorcism and prayer as an in-patient at a private nursing home. He has since done well.'

For several years before the last war Dr McAll supervised a London Mission Hospital in China and, although brought up as a Congregationalist, he now works principally with Anglican and Roman Catholic priests in the Ministry of Deliverance.

In partnership with these priests, he has arranged hundreds of exorcisms in churches. He has also described to me how he has performed many such ceremonies himself in his consulting-room at Lyndhurst, Hampshire – usually with his wife Frances, who is also a doctor.

'There is nothing particularly dramatic about them – except, of course, for the results. I pray with the patient and use a simple form of words, calling on the possessing spirit or power of evil to depart in the name of Jesus Christ. I encourage the patient to follow this up with a communion service in church.'

He also propounds a theory which many may regard as more astonishing than that of demonic possession. He is convinced that people are today being pervaded and are having their health seriously undermined by the souls of babies who have died during abortions or miscarriages – and by the souls of the dead who are unable to find rest because they have not been properly mourned. He claims that, in partnership with priests, he has helped many such people through prayer and exorcism and by arranging special funeral services, without bodies, which are designed to 'commit the earth-bound souls to God'.

One case involved a young girl who had suicidal tendencies and had been suffering for three years with anorexia nervosa. She was too weak to get out of bed when he first saw her.

'Then I discovered a fact which had been kept secret from the girl. Her mother, before marriage, had had an abortion. We said nothing to the patient for she was far too ill to be involved but, having encountered this type of situation often before, I felt I knew the solution. I arranged a church service for the child who had been aborted. Afterwards the mother was crying with relief. She told me that during the service she had actually seen the Lord and that He had told her the baby had been a girl.'

When the daughter was told of the service and the appearance of the Lord, she admitted that she already knew the baby girl who had been calling her by name and asking for help. She went on to say that she had been aware of her unborn sister for years but had never dared mention the fact in case people thought she was mad. She was able to get up shortly afterwards and soon returned to college.

People of all types have benefited from such services. A London businessman was recommended to see Dr McAll in 1979 because he was 'constantly being bugged by unhappy thoughts'.

Two years later when I saw him he said, 'There seemed no logical reason for those thoughts. Everything was running smoothly at the office and at home. I'd had these thoughts off and on for years but they were becoming far worse. I seemed to be living almost permanently under a black cloud and I felt I was heading for a nervous breakdown. Dr McAll questioned me in great detail. He wanted to know about my childhood and parents. Had I ever played around with a ouija-board or been involved in any sort of occult practices? It took him a long time to establish what he believed was probably the cause of my trouble – the fact that there had been two still-born babies during my first marriage. If these children had lived they would by then have been fourteen and nineteen. I must confess that I had more or less forgotten about them because, in my view, they had never really existed. But Dr McAll explained that they were probably still with me – or, at least, their spirits were still with me – and that they were constantly trying to make me aware of them.

'This seemed a bit far-fetched to me for it's hard to grasp the concept of being haunted by one's own children. However, I'd been assured that he knew what he was doing and so, although I wasn't wildly optimistic, I agreed to co-operate. He suggested that I should give each of the children a name, that I should formally recognise their presence, and that I should join him in a service for them. During that service it was as though they were released from my world. I have not been troubled in that way since.'

Testimony of a more dramatic nature has come from a Manchester social worker who described how his wife went to Dr McAll because of similar feelings of inexplicable depression. Dr McAll found that she had had an abortion seven years earlier and tried to persuade her that there should be a service to help the soul of the baby. She was not convinced.

'The next day a shadowy figure appeared at our bedside. My wife said, "If you are my little boy, welcome to the family." The figure sat down beside us and my wife cried. The next day we had a church service for the child. Since then there's been a marvellous change in my wife and our house, which we had believed was haunted, is at peace.'

Yes, maybe it *does* seem far-fetched. But these people have no motive for telling lies on behalf of Dr McAll. They are grateful for his insight and his professional help but they do not regard him particularly as a friend. To them, he is simply the psychiatrist who provided the correct diagnosis and remedy.

If Dr McAll is right these people were being over-shadowed by the dead. And here we have an intriguing parallel with the experience of Joyce Pettigrew in Devon. Her life was being ruined by the spirit of her husband's first wife. Is it not possible that this instance of possession, like many others, was caused partly by the absence of 'proper mourning'? Howard Pettigrew was reluctant to speak ill of Bridget although, through most of their marriage, she had caused him great unhappiness. He suppressed his feelings while she was alive and it is quite conceivable that, however much he might deny the fact, he did not mourn her as whole-heartedly as she would have expected or wished. That absence of deep mourning, following Dr McAll's argument, might have generated angry resentments in her spirit. Can we totally dismiss the possibility that it might also have contributed to her being earth-bound and vengeful?

Here are more cases which Dr McAll reported in the medical journal, *The Lancet*, in August 1980:

> An eleven-year-old girl was involved in a road accident and remained in hospital for many months. When she was discharged from hospital she asked for her father, only to find that he had been killed in the same accident. No family had been present at his funeral. She immediately began to starve herself. By age eighteen she weighed five stone and had been in five hospitals. A local priest arranged a committal service for her father, which she and her mother attended. The following day she felt hungry and started to eat normally. By age twenty-three she had completed a nursing training.
>
> A man of forty-one had been first diagnosed as having anorexia nervosa at age twenty-two. At the time of examination he was not only anorectic but severely depressed. On close questioning he admitted to have precipitated the abortion of his wife's first child. Within a week of this admission and after following through a process of mourning for and committal of the child, he was no longer depressed and was eating normally.

These two cases hardly represent solid evidence in support of Dr McAll's theory. It could well be argued that the remission of the problems in both patients was stimulated simply by removing guilt through the process of mourning. Then it would follow that the problems had been caused by nervous or emotional disorders rather than by possession. It cannot be disputed, however, that the patients were speedily restored to health after the ritual of mourning. The prescribed treatment produced the desired results.

Another of Dr McAll's patients was a young woman teacher who had been certified five times and had been seen by seventeen psychiatrists. Her troubles had flared after the death of a friend with whom, it was eventually discovered, she had had a long-established lesbian relationship. 'None of the other psychiatrists had considered the possibility that she might have become possessed by the spirit of this dead friend,' he told me. 'Yet that's exactly what had happened. Her thinking and her moods were being governed by two separate intelligences between which, all too often, there was disagreement and even antagonism. This was the real cause of her unpredictable behaviour.'

He arranged a church service during which a priest ordered the spirit to leave in the name of Chirst.

'The transformation in my patient was remarkable and immediate. She told me that it felt as if something had flown out of her head and her recovery, from then onwards, progressed well.'

Lunatic violence can also be provoked, he claims, by skeletons in the ancestral cupboard. He firmly believes that people can be infiltrated by the spirits of their forebears and that this type of possession can leapfrog from one individual to another across the centuries. Here are two typical cases of 'ancestor infestation' which he described in *The Expository Times* in July 1975:

> A lady who had been confined in a padded cell had not spoken for two years and had to be forcibly fed by her husband as she violently resisted members of the staff. She had failed to

respond to any treatment. On being approached one day with the suggestion that she was 'demon possessed' she immediately came out with the name of an ancestor and asked to see a priest. This led to her immediate healing and release.

Another lady, also in a padded cell because of her violent attacks, was recognised to be acting out the violence of her sixteenth-century ancestors. It was impossible to communicate with her but at the moment we decided, with her family and church, to hold a service of Eucharist and lay before our Lord the problems of this repeated pattern of family behaviour, at that very moment the patient was cured and became perfectly normal.

Dr David Gill, a consultant psychiatrist at Mapperley Hospital, Nottingham, has made a specialised study of the occult and works closely with a Church of England exorcist. In March 1981 the *Catholic Herald* quoted him as saying:

> 'Unfortunately, our medical schools do not teach doctors except along conditioned, programmed, logical trains of thought. There should perhaps be more training for doctors in the humanities and ethics; taking in anthropology, and parapsychology, and not strait-jacketed to conventional psychology . . . the doctor shouldn't dismiss occult phenomena as superstition . . . or try, inappropriately, to pigeonhole them into a diagnostic category. He should be humble enough to recognise that it may be necessary to involve the priest or minister of religion . . .'

Psychiatrists with that type of 'humility' might well have brought earlier relief to Victoria Bushnell*, of Worthing, a woman in her late sixties who was convinced that for more than thirty years she was victimised by evil which she helped to generate 'several lives ago'. She was not released from this bondage until early in 1981 when she was exorcised by Father Wheaton.

Miss Bushnell gives the impression of being much the same as so many middle-class and comparatively comfortably off people who, after successful careers, have retired to the country or to resorts on the coast. She enjoys pottering in her patch of garden and taking her dog for strolls along the front. She likes making jam and listening to classical music. She is cheerful and friendly and well-liked. There is nothing about her, in fact, to make her neighbours suspect that until the exorcism she had endured a grotesque type of torment and kept it a secret even from her family, because she is ashamed.

'How could I tell them about the times I've deliberately injured myself? They could never start to understand. My parents were very strait-laced and evangelical in their faith. I was brought up to regard regular church attendance as normal and, because my belief was also strong, I was happy to do so. The Church continued to have a central place in my life after I'd left home.'

Lively intelligence and a good education helped her secure an interesting job in the Civil Service and, in time, she was promoted to a supervisory post. 'My work was stimulating and completely absorbing. That was the reason I never married. Don't get the idea that I'm one of those women who have sacrificed themselves to look after their parents. I had plenty of men friends but I was too involved with my career to consider becoming a wife.'

Her life was contented and successful until a November day in 1949. 'I was at a communion service in Westminster Abbey. At the beginning of the service I was fine but suddenly, for no reason that I could fathom, I felt that I couldn't take communion. The idea of doing so seemed repulsive and also vaguely frightening. I started shivering and, when it was my turn to go forward, I turned and almost ran out of the Abbey. I couldn't understand what was wrong with me. I just knew that I had to get out.'

That was the start of a split in her personality. 'From that day on I had a morbid dread of churches. I forced myself to go into them but I always started trembling and weeping. I could never stay to the end of a service and finally I stopped going altogether.'

By then there were other problems.

'I had a feeling that there was more than one person inside me and that these personalities, spirits or whatever, were in conflict. At times one of them seemed to be completely predominant and it was this one which made me do harm to my body. I found I was unable to stop doing idiotic things. I'd take a hotwater bottle and press it tight against my stomach. I didn't want to do it because I hated the pain. I used to get awful blisters and burns but I couldn't stop inflicting this on myself. I tried to pray but the thoughts and words wouldn't come. It was as though there was a battle going on in my mind, with the real me trying to resist the will of some other intelligence. My colleagues in the office, as far as I know, still regarded me as normal and efficient. I often wondered how they'd have reacted if they'd known that, under my clothing, I was bandaged because of my self-inflicted injuries.'

Eventually she consulted her doctor who referred her to a psychiatrist. 'I went on seeing this psychiatrist and others for nearly five years but they couldn't identify what was wrong with me. They had all sorts of magnificent theories. They decided at one stage that I'd been repressed as a child – which, in retrospect, I recognise was probably true – and that my behaviour was a reaction to that repression. One of them took the view that I'd been forced to go to church, possibly against my will, and that was why later I subsconciously rebelled against going. But I'd been so indoctrinated as a girl, according to this man, that I felt guilty over no longer worshipping in church and it was this guilt that made me injure myself as a punishment.

'They seemed very fine and logical, these theories, but they weren't of any practical use. The psychiatrists could give me sedatives but they couldn't give me any real cure. In the end I stopped seeing them. Things hadn't changed. I was still trying to keep up a facade of being normal but I could never step into a church and I still had this terrible compulsion to cause myself pain.'

She endured this condition through the rest of her working life and then, shortly after moving to Worthing, she sought the advice of a clairvoyant.

'She told me that my problem had started in an earlier life. She said that she had a distinct impression of me as I had been in the sixteenth century. I was living then near Windsor in the body of a woman who was involved in witchcraft. I'd been heavily involved in evil during that life and this evil had entered me. It had become absorbed into my spirit and now, in the same spirit, it was affecting my life in this present body.'

So through most of her career as a respected Civil Servant Miss Bushnell, according to this clairvoyant, was serving a form of penance. She was existing in a twentieth-century earthly hell because of her activities, four hundred years earlier, as a witch in Berkshire.

It was this psychic diagnosis – a mistaken one, in my opinion – which finally made Miss Bushnell resolve to seek the aid of an exorcist. Through friends in the West Country, she had heard of the work being done by Father Wheaton and, struggling to suppress her antagonism towards the Christian religion, she arranged to visit him in Exeter.

He invited her to kneel before the altar in the Oratory of Our Lady while he blessed the salt and the water.

All the familiar apprehensions and feelings of distaste were starting to simmer, as she admitted later, as she heard him concentrating first on the salt: 'I exorcise thee, creature of salt, by the living God, by the holy God, by the omnipotent God, that thou mayest be purified from all evil influence, in the name of Him who is Lord of angels and of men, who filleth the whole earth with His majesty and glory. Amen.'

He then offered this prayer: 'We pray thee, O God, in thy boundless loving-kindness to stretch forth the right hand of thy power upon this creature of salt which we bless and hallow in thy holy name. Grant that this salt may make for health of mind and body to all who partake thereof and that there may be banished from the place where it is used every power of adversity and every illusion or artifice of evil; through Christ our Lord. Amen.'

Then he prepared the water with similar words and this was followed by a second prayer: 'O God, who for the helping and safeguarding of men dost hallow the water set apart for the service of Thy holy church, send forth Thy light and Thy power upon this element of water which we bless and hallow in Thy holy name. Grant that whosoever uses this water in faithfulness of spirit may be strengthened in all goodness and that everything sprinkled with it may be made holy and pure and guarded from all assaults of evil; through Christ our Lord. Amen.'

Miss Bushnell was now half regretting having come into this tiny chapel. She had an urge to get up and hurry out, just as she had once left Westminster Abbey, but logic told her to stay. Without this service, she felt, there could be no hope of peace.

Father Wheaton, now casting the salt three times into the water in the form of a cross, was repeating: 'Let salt and water mingle together in the name of the Father and of the Son and of the Holy Ghost. Amen.' He paused and smiled reassuringly at her: 'The Lord be with you.' And, to her surprise, she found herself responding spontaneously: 'And with thy spirit.'

Then she listened, a little more at ease now, while he offered another prayer: 'O God, the giver of invincible strength and king of irresistible power, whose splendour shines throughout the whole of creation, we pray thee to look upon this thy creature of salt and water, to pour down upon it the radiance of thy blessing and to hallow it with the dew of thy loving-kindness, that wherever it shall be sprinkled and thy holy name shall be invoked in prayer, every noble aspiration may be strengthened, every good resolve made firm and the fellowship of the Holy Spirit vouchsafed to us who put our trust in thee; thou who with the Son livest and reignest in the unity of the same Holy Spirit, God throughout all ages of ages.'

This time she joined loudly in the Amen.

After this service, for the first time in more than thirty years, Miss Bushnell was able to take communion. I kept in contact with her afterwards and found that she was again able to enter churches and to take part wholeheartedly in the services. The masochism had gone. But had she *really* been possessed by her own 'witch spirit'?

That explanation strikes me as unlikely and, indeed, I am not entirely convinced that she was possessed by any alien spirit. I feel it is possible that her problems may have stemmed from her subconscious and that the ceremony of exorcism, which drew her emotions up to such a peak, provided the alleviating trigger.

But she *was* released from her torment.

The possibility of her difficulties having been emotional or psychosomatic, rather than spiritual, does not change the key fact: psychiatrists had failed to offer any remedy as effective as that provided by a priest. I totally agree with a comment made by Father Ian Hazlewood: 'Even if we were completely wrong and there was never anything which needed exorcising, at the very least we would do no harm – as long as the ceremonies were conducted within strict guidelines. There is a strong chance that, in appropriate cases, we could be of tremendous help to patients. So would it not be logical for medical people, who have experimented with so many forms of treatment, to consider seriously giving exorcism a chance.'

Medical people should ask themselves the question: 'Is it just possible that there are others suffering at this moment, in their own homes or possibly in mental hospitals, who might be helped in this manner?'

Bigotry should not be allowed to impede the possible recovery of patients. Nor should professional arrogance.

8 Religious fanaticism in America

Impressionable people can be nudged towards dangerously irrational behaviour by freakish ideas about sin and demons now being propounded in Britain. These are ideas which help to generate the types of crazed fanaticism already responsible for a series of horrifying tragedies – including the deaths of children who have been tortured during bizarre ceremonies of so-called exorcism.

Many of the wilder and most disturbing assertions about possession have come from America where religious extremism is more flamboyantly obvious than in Europe, and they are being eagerly endorsed as the 'real truth' by persuasive evangelists and by a number of ordained clergymen in the mainstream churches.

This is causing immense damage. In the minds of many it helps to make religion seem ludicrous, an easy target for derision, and it devalues the work being done by responsible exorcists. In the minds of others, including those who may be emotionally unstable, it can create unhealthy obsessions which, in turn, can lead to disaster.

During my researches I spent time in the English Midlands with a group of lay 'missionaries' – all advocates of exorcism – who were telling huge congregations that 'fleshy activities open the door to Satan'. That did not sound unreasonable – until they defined those 'fleshy activities'. Gluttony, they insisted, is Satanic. No one should make the mistake of regarding it merely as undesirable or unhealthy. It is positively *Satanic.* People who eat too many cakes or sweets are inviting possession by a demon. Laziness and tiredness are not just physical states or attitudes. Both need the rituals of exorcism for they are discarnate spirits of evil.

Overwork, conversely, is a sin because it 'lowers your resistance, friends, and so is an invitation to evil'. A boy who disobeys his parents is not merely being defiant but is controlled by an identifiable entity called a rebellious spirit. Even a dose of influenza, according to these fanatics, can be evidence of an 'attack by Satan'.

Where did they get these extraordinary notions? From a book called *Setting the Captives Free* by Bob Buess, an evangelist in America. It describes a profusion of graphic but anonymous cases of 'deliverance' – such as that of a woman who is said to have terrified her children until the wonderful day when she felt 'demons come out like long snakes'. These demons were trespassing spirits of anger. Mr Buess claims to have exorcised a woman possessed by a spirit of self-pity which, at the peak of the ritual, started yelling defiantly: 'God does not love this woman!'

Accounts of this nature are popular with some of the more aggressively-campaigning cults in the United States. I have heard similar ones from young American evangelists, most of them from California, hot-gospelling in London and other parts of Britain.

The missionaries in the Midlands believe that *Setting the Captives Free* is a work inspired by God. Now they are trying, with some success, to inculcate its attitudes into converts. They mould their own lives on its guide-lines and, as a result, they see demons virtually everywhere.

One of them fervently assured me that the Brownies are a recruiting agency for Satan: 'They betray themselves in so many ways . . . they take small groups of little girls, for example, and call them "sprites". Sprites are water-demons! So these children, in their innocence, are being labelled as workers for the Devil!'

Another saw two demons, masquerading as bats, during a service in a Baptist chapel. How did he know they were not bats?

'Because I exorcised them,' he replied. 'I prayed to Jesus for Him to send them to Hell. And when I opened my eyes they had gone.'

As much of the impetus for this brand of hard-line fanaticism comes from America, it is hardly surprising that America should have witnessed some of its most appalling consequences.

Three-year-old David Weilbacher died in July 1976 at Yakima, Washington, after a prolonged and macabre exorcism. His principal exorcist insisted afterwards that the killing was justified. He said: 'I am not guilty before God.'

In September 1975 David's recently divorced young mother, Debra Weilbacher, was looking for somewhere to live. A former schoolfriend, Lorraine Edwards, took her to an old house in Yakima's South 12th Street. It was a building used as a home and a place of worship by a group of religious fundamentalists, headed by a chubby, fifty-year-old Oklahoman, Leon Cunningham.

He worked as a car salesman and mechanic. He also claimed to be a man of visions. On the anniversary of President Kennedy's assassination he announced that very soon there would be a rearing up of the Antichrist. He had seen it in a vision and the Antichrist would be the reincarnated John Kennedy. Cunningham and his wife Velma had a daughter, Carolyn, 27, living with them and Lorraine Edwards went to live with them after having a child by one of their sons.

This household welcomed Debra and David – after she had promised to pledge herself unquestioningly to God. This meant to God as interpreted by Leon Cunningham. He also had a vision of Texas, where he believed the family would be safe from the 'Kennedy Antichrist'. That was where they ought to live. They began selling their possessions in readiness for the move but, they felt, there was just one problem. There was something peculiar about David. . . .

His 'peculiarity' was first noticed after he had been taken on a walk in the neighbourhood and had seen the blackened ruins of three burned out houses. They fascinated him. In Cunningham's view, that was not normal. Soon there were other indications of 'abnormality'. David would wet himself and smear his excrement on the bathroom walls. He laughed in a disconcertingly adult manner and he seemed to smell differently from other children. One night his mother woke suddenly, believing that David had bitten her on the shoulder. She could not be certain. But she had the *impression* that he had done so. And in the mornings she often found him staring at her. All this seemed so disturbingly unnatural that he was put to bed in another room. It was about then that they recognised the 'truth': the devil had taken possession of the child.

Cunningham believed that all solutions could be found in the Bible. The answer to this problem, in his view, was in Proverbs: 'Withhold not correction from the child: for if thou beatest him with a rod he shall not die. Thou shalt deliver his soul from hell.'

At that stage Debra Weilbacher might well have found other warnings and guidance in Proverbs: 'Avoid a stupid man, you will not hear a word of sense from him . . . a fool at the helm is out of place.' But she would probably have discounted them because she had become hopelessly indoctrinated. Cunningham was the leader. He knew best.

'If thou beatest him with a rod he shall not die. . .'

Those words inspired the ritual thrashings. Twice a day the blond-haired child was taken into a front room to be ceremonially beaten with heavy sticks – by Cunningham, Velma, Carolyn, Lorraine Edwards and his mother. Each would strike several times before passing on the stick. The boy was hit everywhere except around the kidneys and the genitals. The aim was to drive out the devil.

After each of these ceremonies of 'exorcism', Cunningham would sternly ask the boy: 'Do you have love in your heart?'

The child would reply 'Yes'. He would then be ordered to show that love by hugging and kissing Cunningham. But Cunningham believed that these displays of affection were merely a charade. The devil inside the boy, which they could still see in his eyes, was trying to trick them. . .

They persevered. They drove out the devil but, according to Cunningham, David promptly invited it back. They drove it out again and again he called it to repossess him. Cunningham now felt it was necessary to change the ritual. The boy was being stubbornly self-destructive and he had to be humbled. The new ritual involved David being pushed to the floor and then being ordered to stand up. If he failed to do so quickly, he was beaten.

Then he would be pushed down again. Cunningham was confident that this treatment was proving effective. As he stared deep into David's eyes, he felt he could see the devil retreating yet again from its tiny host. But it was still not abandoning him completely.

On the morning of 22 July 1976 David was given another severe beating which was ineffectual and Cunningham decided that the time had come for a major exorcism. That was the will of God.

They performed the major exorcism that afternoon. Again they used sticks and after half-an-hour David collapsed on the floor as if he had fainted. His mother picked him up and, as she did so, they all witnessed a 'demonic attack'. David started to struggle and fight. She lost her grip and he fell heavily to the floor. On his lips were traces of blood and then, still on the floor, he raised his fists and made a noise which sounded like a growl. His chest heaved twice and suddenly he was still.

They saw no need to call a doctor. This was a matter only for God.

They carried his dead body to a bedroom where his mother changed his underclothes. Then they put him on the bed and during the following three days Debra Weilbacher cleansed him with a wet sponge. On the fourth day Cunningham led the entire group into the room and tried to summon life back into the body. All of them said prayers around the bed before Cunningham lifted the body and intoned: 'In the name of Jesus Christ, arise!' He held the body for a while, still hoping for the miracle, before replacing it on the bed.

Cunningham remained convinced that they would witness the miracle. They merely needed patience.

Precautions had to be taken to make certain no demons could enter the room so that David, on his return to life, would be spiritually clean. They painted the windows and stuffed rags into cracks in the walls. They locked the door and sealed it with tape. One of them would be praying continually in the house while the others slept or went about their business. This vigil went on for two months, with no one looking into the room, and it would probably have gone on far longer if neighbours had not become suspicious.

On 19 September Police Sergeant Robert Langdale arrived at the house and, not satisfied with the replies to his questions, he broke down the door of the back bedroom. The smell was so foul that he had to get a gas-mask.

A pathologist said later that David had probably been beaten to death. He could not be certain, however, because of the state of the body.

Debra Weilbacher spoke of that 'resurrection room' when she appeared before a jury at Yakima County Superior Court: 'Whoever opened that door, I didn't know what they'd find . . . a decomposed body, a little boy, or if they'd find nothing. The day he died, I put him in the back room. I didn't check to see if he was breathing. I knew that God said he wouldn't die.'

She insisted, even then, that David would be restored by God: 'He'll look like David but he won't have a heart like David's.'

Was she sorry that David had died? She paused before agreeing that she was. She was shown a picture of the child. Did it show evil? 'You can't see it in a picture,' she replied. 'But he has a smart look on his face . . . he wanted to hurt everybody. He could think a lot higher than I could think. He'd go into a trance and look at you like you weren't there at all.'

On 8 December 1976 she was found guilty of manslaughter and second-degree assault and was sentenced to ten years in prison for each crime. So were Leon Cunningham and his daughter Carolyn – with Judge Howard Hettinger recommending that Cunningham should serve the entire twenty years. Mrs Cunningham and Lorraine Edwards were each given five years for second-degree manslaughter and ten years for second-degree assault.

After hearing his sentence, Cunningham said: 'I'm not guilty before God. He will judge me.'

*   *   *

*   *   *

In September 1978 a jury at Jasper, Arkansas, was shocked by evidence of how another mother – 22-year-old Goldie Hall – had helped 'exorcise' her three-year-old child to death. The victim was Stephanie Hall and four members of a fanatical religious cult were already serving long sentences for her murder. Goldie Hall had been watching, nodding approvingly, during the grisly ritual which ended in death. She pleaded having been completely under the influence of the cult but was jailed for five years for second-degree murder.

Like David Weilbacher, this little girl had been brutally beaten to rid her of a 'devil'. She had also been burned – 'to feel the heat of Hell' – over a fire on which members of the cult had placed her favourite doll. But this 'devil' had also been tenacious and it was felt that drastic measures were essential to help cleanse the world of evil. Those measures involved taking the toddler to a lonely spot, shooting her eight times, stuffing her into a plastic bag and burying her in a shallow grave.

The cult was called the Church of God in Christ through the Holy Spirit Inc.

* * *
* * *

Five days before Police Sergeant Robert Langdale discovered the body of David Weilbacher another young mother was facing a charge of murder – after the 'exorcism killing' of her son. She was Melissa Norris of Montgomery, Alabama, who was said to have punched, shaken and choked the child, Demiko Loo Norris, to 'rid him of a demon'. Demiko had died on 11 April. He was aged three months.

In March 1977 28-year-old Joyce Lillian Pope was jailed because of the killing which had happened in her home. She was convicted of child abuse and of misprision of a felony (having failed to report another's crime). In a tape-recorded statement to the police, she said that Mrs Norris referred to herself as God while beating the baby whom she addressed as Satan. She told a judge at Montgomery County Circuit Court that during the fatal beating she could not move or do anything to protect the child. She added: 'I knew she was hurting the baby but it was as if there was a shield between us.' The judge sentenced her to two concurrent seven-year terms, with all but eighteen months suspended, and ordered that she be given psychiatric treatment.

And Mrs Norris? She was found not guilty because of insanity.

How many killings of this nature – or, indeed, near-killings – might be traced back to the rantings of evangelical fanatics? How deeply do their extravagant statements about demonology affect people who are already on an emotional or psychiatric seesaw? How often are they indirectly responsible, in fact, for the balance being tilted towards tragedy? It is too simplistic to say that insanity is insanity and that there the matter rests. Ideas which may be analysed and possibly discarded by a rational person can so easily start to smoulder in a disturbed mind. I know one mentally-ill woman whose behaviour pattern changed, to the bewilderment of her family, after she had listened to a song on the radio. She suddenly got into the habit of tearing up banknotes and pushing them in the dustbin to make the world a better place. The song was the well-known one about money being 'the root of all evil'. This woman lives in a London suburb. Her case illustrates a key point: vulnerable people are likely to be triggered into unexpected actions by views they find convincing. Debra Weilbacher was clearly an inadequate. But she would not have helped to kill her own child if she had not been brainwashed by a zealot like Cunningham. That Englishman who identified the Baptist chapel bats as demons – is he not potentially almost as dangerous as Cunningham? I am not suggesting that he would be party to beating a child to death. But his mania about demons, his constant assertions that they swarm in almost every cranny, could help put the susceptible on the path to disaster. His persuasive eloquence can make others start to see demons everywhere and, in some instances, the possible consequences cannot be predicted.

Maybe there is something just a little unusual about a particular individual, something indefinably off-key about his or her personality, and suddenly, to the easily influenced person, the cause may seem obvious: the 'unnaturalness' is being created by a demon which must be driven out.

* * *

* * *

Patricia Abraham, an unmarried mother living in Harlem, New York, identified a 'lurking demon' inside her 18-month-old son, Leon.

Leon's father, Leroy Justin, sobbed with horror when he first heard the full story from the police. It seemed so grotesquely unbelievable. . .

For some time before the killing Miss Abraham had been worried about Leon. He seemed to be getting progressively smaller and, as she put it, he was 'starting to shrink'. Doctors at New York Hospital later confirmed that Leon had been getting thinner because he was undernourished. In fact, he was starving. But Miss Abraham felt she knew the real cause: Leon was wasting away because of a possessing demon. He had to be saved and it was her duty, as his mother, to take the necessary action.

On New Year's Eve, 1979, she went to a party with Leroy Justin and told him she was going to 'drive the devil out of my house for the New Year'. She did not elaborate and, when he left for his own home, he did not feel the comment had any sinister significance.

Later that evening neighbours were disturbed by chanting and 'weird screams'. At about 11.30 pm Miss Abraham pushed her elder son – six-year-old Vance – out of the apartment. She and the boy were naked.

Charles Majette, a neighbour, reported: 'She dragged him back inside and then pushed both Leon and Vance out. We took the kids into a room here but she came out, naked, and said "Where are my boys?"' She then took the children back to her apartment and the neighbours called the police. Almost immediately, they also called the Fire Department because they could smell smoke. They could also hear Miss Abraham shrieking an invitation: 'If you want to see the devil burn, come on in. My baby is saved. The devil is coming out of this baby tonight.'

There was some delay before the arrival of the police, a fact which later caused criticism. The firemen were the first to reach the apartment. Miss Abraham tried to refuse them entry. They were not needed, she insisted, because there was nothing wrong. Smoke? Yes, there had been a bit of a fire because the children had been playing with matches. But it had not been serious and, anyway, it was all over.

Soon after midnight the firemen broke in to find clothes still burning in the bathroom. They also found scraps of clothing on the kitchen stove. Leon was in a bedroom, badly burned, and in the oven were small pieces of flesh. And, eventually, the authorities were able to establish the truth about the nightmare ordeal of this baby boy.

His mother had initially tried to scald the demon out of him with boiling water. She and Vance were both naked during the 'ceremony'; her mother, also present, was wearing a nightgown. After the scalding, she had pushed the nude child into the heated oven.

Leon had second and third degree burns over 95 per cent of his body. Five days later he died of cardiac arrest. Miss Abraham was accused of murder.

In October 1981 a Manhattan Supreme Court judge ruled that she was 'not responsible for reason of mental defect'.

But what had placed the idea of a demon into her tragically-deluded mind? And why should she believe it could be exorcised through burning?

Psychiatrists considering those questions may feel there is a possible link with the 'exorcism' of little Stephanie Hall. That case attracted widespread publicity when Stephanie's mother was convicted in September 1978 and there were descriptions of how the child had been burned 'to feel the heat of Hell'.

Leon was two months at the time. Miss Abraham was at a stage where she was likely to be vulnerable and impressionable because of post-natal depression. Might not a newspaper account of the Arkansas 'exorcism' have sown a seed – one which germinated and flourished because of her susceptibility? Did it make her start to brood, in her confused state, on the possibility that her new illegitimate baby was also infested by a demon?

Leon was the victim of her madness. It is also likely, I suggest, that his agony was inspired by that far-away cult of fanatics.

* * *

* * *

When the film *The Exorcist*, based on the best-seller by William Peter Blatty, was released in 1973 many exorcists reported an upsurge in the number of people who considered themselves to be possessed. This conviction threatened to reach such epidemic proportions in parts of Britain that priests volunteered for extra duties. They arranged to be present at screenings, occasionally on a roster basis, to provide help and reassurance.

The spectacular box office success of the film continued through the 1970s – through the years which brought a series of horrifyingly misguided attempts at exorcism – and in 1980 the American trade paper *Variety* placed it fourth in the list of top-grossing films ever produced. It was one of the very few feature films designed deliberately to invade the subconscious minds of audiences by the use of subliminal images. These were carried on a single frame of film which stayed on the screen for one twenty-fourth of a second. One of these frames showed a priest's face distorted to look like a death-mask. Others showed the word 'pig'. These images were projected far too briefly to be consciously identified by audiences but still made a disturbing impact.

Many of the priests concerned were unaware of this subliminal 'invasion' but merely felt that the film gave a distorted and sensationalised impression of exorcism. It also ignited unnecessary fears, they claimed, by conditioning large numbers of people, especially youngsters, into accepting some of the more lurid concepts of demonology. In their view it was directly responsible for many distressing cases of pseudo-possession. Yet none of them could deny that Blatty's story was based on truth.

His novel was the story of a possessed girl, Regan MacNeill, who was eventually exorcised by a Jesuit. The genuine affair began on 15 January 1949, in a suburb of Washington where a 14-year-old boy started hearing an inexplicable scratching sound around his bed. It continued night after night until on 29

January one of his aunts died in St Louis. The boy and his grandmother then began wondering if the noise might have some connection with her death and, when it started again, they asked: 'Is that you, Aunt Tillie? If it is, knock three times.' They then heard three loud knocks.

Very soon the boy was being scratched while in bed, with marks that appeared to spell out words. Psychologists are understandably reluctant to accept such 'stigmata' signs as an indication of any external spiritual influence. They point out, quite correctly, that these can be created by the mind. Stigmata type swellings can occasionally be seen on the bodies of the mentally ill, for instance, and a person under hypnosis can display blisters when told that a pencil touching him is really a red hot iron. However, there were other phenomena. Bed clothes would suddenly rear up and stand stiffly as if starched. Objects would be hurled around.

The family were Lutherans and on 17 February the pastor of their church took the boy into his own home. There he saw the boy's bed vibrating before the mattress began to undulate violently. He also saw a chair, with the boy seated on it, move across a room and rise a few inches up a wall. It seemed to him that psychiatrists might be able to suggest some solution and so the boy was taken to Georgetown University's Medical Centre. The psychiatrists were also baffled and, with no change in the boy's condition, the pastor advised the family to consult a Catholic priest.

The boy went back to his home which was blessed on 9 March by the priest who also pinned a relic of St Mary Margaret to the head of the boy's bed. And, whilst he was still there, the bed began to move. The following night brought another alarming attack, during which the relic was ripped from the bed and hurled at a mirror.

On 11 March the boy was blessed with a relic of St Francis Xavier and was moved to the Jesuit residence at St Louis. Father William Bowden, pastor of the Collegiate Church of St Louis, and two other priests were authorised to perform an exorcism.

It was apparently a long and arduous exorcism, lasting all night, during which the boy shouted obscenities, chattered in strange languages and was violent. By the next day, however, he was considered clear. He is now a successful businessman, married with three children.

So this is the case, reported later by the Catholic Truth Society, which Batty used as a springboard for his dive into the realms of imagination. His version *was* far more sensational and some of it, to those who have studied exorcism, was totally unbelievable. His fictional exorcist initiated his own destruction by challenging the demon to 'try something bigger' – by inviting it to leave the child and take him instead. Another priest gave an identical invitation in *Amityville 2* – a 1982 film so packed with contrived horrors that it bordered on farce; he was also shown as a victim. Such a cardinal error would hardly be made by an authorised Roman Catholic exorcist who, according to the Vatican-approved Rules, 'must be properly distinguished for his piety, prudence and integrity of life'.

Blatty was merely using literary licence to create the utmost impact in a work of fiction. But, at the same time, the concern of priests in Britain – and elsewhere – was well-founded. Demons were suddenly 'in fashion' because of *The Exorcist*. People were quicker to imagine them, or to see symptoms which 'identified' them. Parents were prepared to accept that unusual behaviour in their children, which previously might have been regarded as a character or health defect, could be a sign of possession. The American exorcism tragedies which I have described happened a comparatively short time after the release of the film. That pattern was also seen on the other side of the Atlantic.

* * *
* * *

Two Roman Catholic priests conducted one of the most horrifying officially-sanctioned exorcisms of this century – shortly after cinemas started screening *The Exorcist*. This was in the Bavarian town of Klingenberg where a young woman died because she and her parents shared the priests' fanaticism on the subject of possession.

In August 1976 West Germans could hear on their radios a series of ear-splitting screams, shouts of '*Heil*' and a muttering of Latin prayers – interspersed by foul language being shouted by an hysterical woman.

They were listening to some of the forty-three tape recordings then in the possession of the state prosecutor, Dr Karl Stenger, who was inquiring into the fate of a student teacher, Anneliese Michel. She had died of malnutrition and exhaustion on 1 July after undergoing nine months of exorcism – with two Roman Catholic priests trying, they explained, to rid her of demons, which included the spirits of Adolf Hitler, the Roman emperor Nero and Judas Iscariot. The recordings had been made by her principal exorcist.

Anneliese was the second of five daughters born into the family of a wealthy timber merchant. From her attic bedroom she could see in the town cemetery the black headstone over her sister Martha who had died at the age of eight in 1956. Martha had been born with three breasts and, according to neighbours, her deeply religious parents regarded this deformity as a mark of the Devil. This belief was to have a lasting effect on Anneliese.

In 1969 she began to have fits and to suffer severe depression. A psychiatrist eventually diagnosed her illness as epilepsy. In 1973 she went to Wurzburg University. A friend found her kneeling naked in her room before a makeshift font which she filled with holy water brought back from a pilgrimage to Rome. She was said to be then in a trance-like state, talking to invisible people or entities.

The first attempt to exorcise her was made by her own parish priest. She became terrified and tore her rosary apart. She also cursed him in strange guttural voices.

In 1975 she gave up seeking medical help and put her trust entirely in the church. That was when the two exorcists began their marathon battle against the 'demons'. For month after month, three days a week,they had sessions with her lasting five hours. She was kept in her attic which was lit by two candles and the exorcists often had to hold her down as she clawed at them in terror. During these sessions she also screamed at the sight of prayer books and a crucifix. She cursed and blasphemed. She thrashed around wildly and battered her head against the walls. And the older of the two priests taped her groans and her strange-voiced rantings, such as the message which he insisted came from the spirit of Hitler: '*Heil!* The bitch belongs to me. Go away!'

Eventually Anneliese, totally demented, stopped eating and drinking. Her parents later claimed the demons had forbidden her to take nourishment and although she was wasting away, neither they nor the priests felt it right to call in medical help.

The senior priest also claimed that the Roman Catholic ritual barred priests carrying out an exorcism from burdening themselves with medical matters. Yet the third of the Roman Catholic General Rules Concerning Exorcism says the priest 'should not believe too readily that a person is possessed by an evil spirit; but he ought to ascertain the signs by which a person possessed can be distinguished from one who is suffering from some illness, especially one of a psychological nature'.

When Anneliese died on 1 July she weighed just under five stone. Even after her burial she was not allowed to rest in peace. A nun claimed that the body had been miraculously preserved in its casket and, early the following year, her parents won the right to have her exhumed. After the exhumation, the authorities issued a terse statement saying that the body showed 'normal decay for its time in the ground'.

In April 1978 the priests were given six-month suspended prison sentences for manslaughter. They were still adamant, however, that they had been right: 'I acted according to my conscience and my belief,' and 'I was convinced then, and still am, that she was possessed by the devil. She died willingly to atone for the sins of others.'

Such sanctimonious and outrageously uncompromising attitudes are far more common than is generally realised and have now permeated mainstream churches in Britain. .

9 Religious fanaticism in Britain

Has any member of your family, living or dead, been addicted to tobacco? Has any one of them admitted to being superstitious? If you answer 'yes' to either of those questions, you should make a formal confession as a matter of urgency. Otherwise, you are in danger of becoming possessed.

Did one of your grandfathers try dowsing for water? Do you have an aunt, or even a distant cousin, who has experimented with telepathy? Once again, if the answers are 'yes' you could well be at risk.

This may savour of the rantings one might expect from certain fundamentalists in fringe cults. In fact, they are warnings being given seriously within the Church of England. They form part of an 'occult check list' – purporting to explain causes of 'contamination' – which one vicar uses to strike fear into his parishioners.

He was most unhappy to learn that I had obtained a copy of this duplicated document from his country church – although it was freely available there – and he begged not to be identified. 'My bishop doesn't know I use it,' he explained. 'I'm not really sure that he'd approve . . .'

The explanatory notes start: 'The Occult Realm is far more extensive than is usually appreciated by Christians. Satanic activity is a constant problem to us – "he prowls around like a roaring lion" – and while some activities are occult in themselves, others are used by Satan to bring us into bondage.'

This vicar is far from being the only cleric in Britain so besotted by demonology and his 'occult check list' demonstrates how irrationality can be fostered in our churches – bringing with it potential dangers for the emotionally-unsteady.

It can help convince them that they – or someone close to them – have been entered by demons. It can encourage them into seeking unnecessary exorcisms which could end in disaster.

The explanatory notes continue: 'He (Satan) involves us in his dark realm by – a) Our witting or unwitting participation in what is utterly forbidden in Scriptures; b) By aiding and abetting our sins; c) By the visitation of the sins of the fathers upon us the children.

If you watch an unsuitable television programme, according to this vicar, you would become a target for demons. You could also become a target without seeing that programme. The backlash could be just as severe against you, he claims, if it were watched in their own homes by any of your blood relatives.

Here are samples of the questions which he says can help you assesss your own spiritual jeopardy:

Have you or any members of your family, living or dead, had handwriting analysed by an expert? Have any of you kept good-luck charms or 'oriental ornaments that have occult or religious significance'? Have you been hypnotised or had acupuncture?

The vicar believes that your answers will show how far you have already gone towards embracing Satan.

It is also psychically hazardous to be 'addicted to medically prescribed drugs' or to be 'under an anaesthetic in the hands of a medical person who is a practising spiritualist', to visit a Hindu temple or even to read about 'paranormal subjects'. The list goes on and on – making life seem rather like a demon-filled game of snakes and ladders.

Have you ever been harassed by gipsies? Have you ever had a serious illness or been involved in a car accident? Was your mother ill while carrying you? These are just some of the eventualities alleged to put you in spiritual danger.

Many of these questions would appear to be aimed at children, for special mention is made in the document of how psychic dangers can stem from *sounds* which may be heard at school.

The vicar believes: 'Satan is utterly adept at using points of "infection" to inflict further damage if we are not cleansed and healed by the Lord, through discernment of our counsellors or teachers.'

Counsellors or teachers? In his parish this means himself and any members of the laity he may nominate.

The document concludes with the following instruction: 'This check list should be burned or otherwise destroyed after healing has been ministered following confession, absolution and renunciation.'

I have refrained from naming this vicar for it is not my wish to cause him distress. However, I would advise any reader presented with such a document to regard it with grave suspicion – and to question the credibility of its author. A man's judgement on matters spiritual should not be accepted automatically because he is a vicar. That fact was demonstrated in the most horrendous way by the case of Michael Taylor.

People at Ossett, near Barnsley, knew Taylor as a cheerful and gentle man. He lived contentedly with his wife, Christine, and their five sons. A friend described him as 'a devoted father and loving husband for whom marriage was one long courtship'. That courtship ended in the most harrowing way imaginable in October 1974 when he underwent a night-long form of exorcism.

Four hours after that ceremony in the vestry of a church – during which dozens of evil spirits, including those of incest and bestiality, were believed to have been expelled – he killed his beloved Christine. He gouged out her eyes, ripped out her tongue, clawed away part of her face. Then he walked naked through the streets near his home covered with what he called 'the blood of Satan'. Only thirteen days earlier, according to a consultant psychiatrist, he had been 'a stable, intelligent, hard-working young man with no signs of mental illness'.

The first step towards the transformation of Michael Taylor, who had previously shown virtually no interest in religion, came on 24 September when he and Christine played host to members of a Christian Fellowship Group. Those present included a lay preacher, Marie Robinson, to whom Taylor had been introduced in the July. She administered holy communion, although she was not ordained, and she was later quoted as saying: 'I suppose you could call me a sort of normal Jesus freak.'

At another group meeting in the Taylors' home, on 27 September, Miss Robinson began speaking in tongues. She also performed an exorcism on another member of the group and suddenly Taylor, in a highly-charged state of fervour, also began uttering glossolalia. His personality was already starting to disintegrate. By 2 October Taylor was telling neighbours and his mother that he had seen the devil who had ordered him to kill himself. Miss Robinson visited the house again that day and, she said later, she was terrified when attacked by Taylor.

This outbreak of violence had come shortly after Taylor had kissed her while his wife was in another room. Hugging was an accepted expression of friendship between members of the Christian Fellowship. It was a sign of unity in the sight of God. However, she considered that this kissing was different.

At the inquest on Mrs Taylor, she said: 'Mike called me to sit next to him. I sat on the floor. Mike said 'I know the way you feel about me.' He had it in his mind that I was attracted to him. He is a good-looking man and I must have shown this to him. He kissed me. As he kissed me the whole of my being just reacted completely against it. I felt a clash of wills, a clash of spirits. I said to him, 'If you love Christ don't try anything. It is wrong against the Lord.' He then said to me, 'I know. We have got to fight this thing.'

'When Chris came into the room he said to her, "We have won a great victory for the Lord. A miracle has happened. We have both overcome our passions." '

Christine Taylor had not seen them kissing but she had found them embracing and, according to Miss Robinson, she knew that her husband had a potential emotional involvement. She knew that his love for Miss Robinson was more than platonic and she began to tell him so.

Miss Robinson continued: 'I suddenly glanced at Mike and his whole features seemed to have changed. He looked almost bestial. He kept looking at me and there was a really wild look in his eyes. I started screaming at him out of fear. I did not know what to say. I started speaking in a tongue . . . Mike also screamed at me in a tongue. We just screamed at each other. He started slapping my face. Chris tried to push him off. Somehow we were at the other side of the room. I don't know whether Mike had dragged me or pushed me or what. I realised we were at the other side of the room with him crouching over me ready to kill. It was like pictures of lions ready to kill their prey. I really tasted fear in my mouth. I thought I was on the verge of death. I knew that only the name of Jesus could save me and I just started saying over and over again "Jesus". I believe it was only by calling his name that I was saved.'

This incident was also described to another member of the Fellowship Group by Taylor who said that, although they were both fully clothed, he and Miss Robinson appeared to each other as naked.

Talking later to a police inspector, he said: 'I saw her standing naked before me and I was naked too. She was looking and her eyes became slits. I felt evil with me. I fought it – but it overcame me. I had sought knowledge of myself and my being on earth and she tried to give it to me but this is not the way. She was wrong and they were all wrong. They tried to bring me peace of mind but instead they filled me with the devil. They tried – oh, how they tried – but it was too late. I had to destroy . . . '

On 3 October Taylor attended another meeting of the Fellowship Group at the home of the choirmaster of St Thomas's Church in Gawber, a village near Barnsley. Those present included the Reverend Peter Vincent, the vicar of Gawber, who had been part of a team at earlier exorcisms. It was decided that Taylor should make his confession and be granted absolution. By this time he was eating very little and was having virtually no sleep. The disintegration of his personality was accelerating.

On 4 October he made Christine throw all religious books and three crosses out of their home. He insisted on having the radio on throughout the night because he was afraid of the silence.

On the afternoon of 5 October another member of the Fellowship Group, John Eggins, took the Taylor family for a drive in the country.

Suddenly Taylor screamed. The others decided to drive

immediately to St Thomas's vicarage at Gawber. When they arrived Taylor was noisy, irrational and violent. He kept pacing around, rubbing his hands, and occasionally he pushed his handkerchief into his mouth to rid himself, he said, of the taste of holy communion. Twice he was offered bacon, eggs and coffee. On both occasions he started to eat but spat the food out and knocked over the coffee. He attacked Vincent and threw a cat out of the window. Vincent said that there was then a strong feeling that Taylor was possessed. 'But we wanted to be absolutely certain of this by what we call the word of the Lord. The means by which we ascertain the will of the Lord was that used by Gideon in the Book of Judges – putting down a fleece.'

This was a reference to Judges 6 which, in *The New English Bible*, reads: 'Gideon said to God, "I am putting a fleece of wool on the threshing floor. If there is dew only on the fleece and all the ground is dry, then I shall be sure that thou wilt deliver Israel through me . . ." '

Vincent said, 'We could not do this in a literal sense but adopted the same procedure. In Michael's case we believed if we asked an evil spirit to name itself we would have thought and prayed for further guidance.'

In fact, according to Vincent, a spirit – using Taylor's voice – did respond immediately and identified itself as incest.

Geoffrey Baker, prosecuting, took up the story at Leeds Crown Court after Taylor had pleaded not guilty: 'There were ample signs at that time that this man was mentally unstable and, indeed, it is put beyond all doubt by the vicar's wife, Mrs Vincent, who said that within a few minutes of his arrival she took the view that Taylor was irrational and no longer in control of his faculties. She went on to say that there was an enormous force of evil emanating from Taylor and in her view this was a difficult case of demon possession and it required an exorcism which was going to be a long job – probably all night. Her husband shared that view. However, Mrs Vincent felt that other people, experienced in exorcism, ought to be summoned and she telephone around for assistance.

'Among people who responded to the call were the Reverend Raymond Smith, a Barnsley Methodist minister and his wife

Margaret, who described themselves as practitioners in exorcism. In addition, there came to the house a Methodist lay preacher, Donald James, and they spent some time, as they called it, "counselling" Taylor – asking him questions, finding out the answers and putting suggestions to him . . . It is perhaps astonishing in this day and age that they all came to the conclusion that Taylor was demonically possessed by Satan, by a strong force of evil which required nothing more or less than prolonged exorcism . . .

'There was one dissenting voice. The Reverend Smith, to his credit, said that God was telling him that Michael Taylor really needed to be in a psychiatric unit. This suggestion was considered. It was solemnly rejected. The Reverend Vincent said they wished to continue with the exorcism. It is a thousand pities that all those assembled in the vicarage at that time did not at once on the Saturday evening summon medical aid.'

At midnight Taylor was taken into the vestry of the church. Windows were opened so that expelled demons could leave.

Baker continued: 'They laid him on hassocks on the floor and at times they had to hold him down. They took it in turns to exorcise each particular demon, as they put it, as it was called out. The account they give is unbelievable. It is difficult for those who read it, and for you who have to listen to it, to believe that you are not back in the Middle Ages. They made a list of the spirits as they named themselves and they spoke of casting out spirits one by one – the spirits of incest, bestiality, blasphemy, heresy, lewdness, masochism and many others. They knew, they say, that each spirit had been expelled because Taylor had breathed out or expelled his breath violently.

'At some time during the night the view was taken that the cross which had been given to him by Miss Robinson and which he was wearing round his neck on a leather thong was cursed by Satanic influences and so they took the wooden cross and burned it. His wife's silver cross was taken and buried in the ground. It seems that at the same time as the exorcism of Taylor his wife was also having spirits exorcised in the vicarage because she is alleged to have felt the presence of Satan within her.

'This exorcism lasted all night and at 6 am they had reached the stage where Mrs Smith, wife of the Reverend Raymond Smith, said that at least forty demons had been cast out and had left Michael Taylor. Taylor and those allegedly ministering to him were exhausted and at about 7 am Taylor, according to Mrs Vincent, the vicar's wife, had three demons left in him – insanity, murder and violence. They had not been expelled yet. According to Mr Eggins, who was there at the church, they could not be called forth. According to Mr James, the lay preacher, he said that only the spirit of murder remained and could not be expelled.'

Mrs Margaret Smith said God had told her that, if Taylor went home that morning, he would murder his wife and children.

Baker continued: 'Those gathered there decided then that psychiatric treatment was necessary. They did make efforts to contact a mental welfare officer but were not successul.'

West Yorkshire police were contacted and they advised that this was a matter for the medical profession. Christine Taylor refused to allow a call to be made to the family doctor. She feared that this would anger her husband.

It is possible in certain circumstances for the police to make an arrest before an offence has been committed, and I am confident that, if the police had been in possession of all the facts, the necessary steps would have been taken to protect the Taylor family. Detective Chief Superintendent Sills said later that the police had been given very few details and that he was satisfied they had done all they could.

Christine Taylor agreed that the children should go into the care of their grandparents but she refused to be parted from her demented husband – insisting that she would be protected by Christ.

Eggins drove Michael and Christine Taylor to their home. At 9.30 am Christine Taylor told a neighbour: 'Don't come near me because there is something in me.'

At 9.45 she went out again and commented that her husband needed a doctor but that they were going to have a good rest. At ten o'clock she was murdered and partially mutilated. Taylor also wrung the neck of the family poodle. At 10.45 the police found Taylor naked in the street. He was wearing his wife's gold rings and his body was covered with blood.

Baker said: 'He was on his hands and knees with his forehead touching the ground. When the police officer asked him where all that blood had come from me he said, "It is the blood of Satan."

'Mr Taylor later told the police: "I have killed my wife. I know I have. It came through religion. They primed me for this last night."

'In a statement which was read out later Mr Taylor said: "I had to destroy. I am relaxed now. I am at peace. It was terrible. They had me in the church all night. Look at my hands. I was banging them on the floor. The power was in me. I could not get rid of it and neither could they." '

How was this connected with his wife's death? 'I was compelled by the force within me which they couldn't get rid of. I felt compelled to destroy everything in the house. Everything, including the dog.'

Consultant psychiatrist Dr Hugo Milne, called for the defence, said that at the time of the killing Taylor was insane but that, shortly afterwards he was 'clinically and legally sane'. During the ceremony of exorcism, said Milne, Taylor was 'demonstrating what I know as a condition of hyper-ventilation. This is described as the spirits leaving his body and this physiological process in any normal human being is in itself dangerous. If you breathe repeatedly and quickly you alter your consciousness and can behave in an aggressive and uncontrolled way.'

On 25 March 1975 the Leeds jury returned a special verdict on Michael Taylor: 'Not guilty of murder by reason of insanity.' By that time he was again sane but, under the 1964 Criminal Procedure (Insanity) Act, Mr Justice Caulfield had to commit him to Broadmoor. That was the only sentence permitted by law on such a verdict.

Broadmoor was opened in 1863 as an 'asylum for criminal lunatics'. That hurtful description has now been banned. Within the terms of the 1959 Mental Health Act, it became a 'special hospital' for 'persons who require treatment under conditions of special security on account of their dangerous, violent or criminal propensities'. So this was the place to which the judge had to send a totally sane individual. Three years later Michael Taylor, his release sanctioned by the Home Secretary, was trying to rebuild his shattered life as a free man.

And what was the attitude, after the killing, of the Reverend Peter Vincent? At the inquest he refused to accept that the exorcism had been 'a grotesque and hideous failure'. He very much regretted what had happened but said: 'I am convinced that God will bring good out of this in His own way, however tragic it was at the time.'

* * *
* * *

Leaders of the fundamental charismatic movement, which is attracting increasing support from members of all the Christian churches, are almost unanimously in favour of exorcism. Their practice of speaking in tongues – with God supposedly talking to them and through them – is described in the Acts of the Apostles, Act 2, verses 3 to 6:

> And there appeared to them tongues like flames of fire, dispersed among them and resting on each one. And they were all filled with the Holy Spirit and began to talk in other tongues, as the Spirit gave them power of utterance. Now there were living in Jerusalem devout Jews drawn from every nation under heaven; and at this sound the crowd gathered, all bewildered because each one heard his own language spoken.

Act 10, verses 44 to 46:

> Peter was still speaking when the Holy Spirit came upon all who were listening to the message. The believers who had come with Peter, men of Jewish birth, were astonished that the gift of the Holy Spirit should have been poured out even on the Gentiles. For they could hear them speaking in tongues of ecstasy and acclaiming the greatness of God.

Speaking in tongues has been a recurring feature of religious revivals since the Middle Ages. Some of the early Quakers and Methodists were reported to have spoken in tongues. There was a big revival in America early this century under the name Pentecostalism and now it is being accepted by a growing number of priests within the orthodox churches in Britain.

The fervency of the charismatic movement is undeniably winning converts to Christianity but many of its adherents are too arrogantly confident of their own infallibility. They are contemptuous of attitudes and disciplines associated with what they call 'Churchianity'. They tend to be religious mavericks and there is often a danger that their unsupervised exorcisms may end in tragedy.

Beatrix Rutherford first met a former actor called John Sherwood – a charismatic who was commonly known as John the Preacher – at a bus stop in Victoria, London. She had a history of mental instability. He was an evangelist who roamed the world in search of converts and often preached in Hyde Park. It was a chance meeting which was to lead to horror. Within a few weeks Beatrix Rutherford was dead, having suffered appalling injuries during a misguided attempt at exorcism.

At one time Sherwood had been a house-parent at a children's home run by Wandsworth Council in London. He started to embrace fanatical beliefs in 1977 after seeing a play about religion. He sold virtually all his possessions so that he could devote his life to his new concept of Christianity. On two occasions he was arrested while evangelising abroad for not having proper visas.

A few weeks after the encounter at Victoria, he walked into the police station at Edmonton in suburban London and made a statement: 'I have killed a woman trying to get devils out of her. I used too much force. I wasn't hitting her. I was hitting devils. I didn't mean to kill her. I loved her. I hoped to rid her soul of oppression, condemnation and suffering. It's not in my nature to do this. I'm not fit to live. Spirits were manifesting themselves and controlling her face. It was filled with evil which kept showing itself. She was groaning but it wasn't her voice. It was another voice. The situation escalated from a gentle rebuke to physical force, not against Beatrix but against the devil which I thought was manifesting itself in her body . . . I didn't realise the pain I was causing her.' He also asked to see the pastor of the Pentecostal church where he had been praying before the killing.

Beatrix Rutherford was already known to the police because she had made several false confessions of murder. One of her cousins, a Roman Catholic nun, was later to testify that Beatrix had claimed to be a black witch and that, apart from believing herself to be a mass murderess, she considered herself responsible for radiating evil. She had become a voluntary patient at a psychiatric hospital after the breakdown of a nine-year lesbian affair. The police were well aware that she was a pathetic and inadequate person. They also soon learned a great deal about this bearded evangelist and about his partner in the horrendous exorcism, Anthony Strover. They had met while preaching in Hyde Park and were members of a sect known as the Invisible Church, which was based in Richmond, Surrey.

Sherwood moved into Beatrix's flat in Park Road, Edmonton – opposite the New Testament of God Pentecostal Church – soon after their meeting.

Her former lesbian partner, with whom she had kept in contact, visited the flat a few hours before the exorcism. David Tudor Price, for the prosecution at the Old Bailey, said she was let in by Sherwood and she found that Beatrix was 'in a poor mental state and was crying'. The woman was distressed by what she saw and she was taken out by Sherwood who advised her to read the Scriptures.

This woman told the jury that when she first met Sherwood she thought he was 'like a Mormon off a wagon train. His beard was long and he looked just like a preacher such as you see in wagon train serials.'

She had seen Beatrix a month before the exorcism and she had then seemed well. On the day of her death, however, Beatrix had not seemed the same person. Her head was bound, her hair was filthy and she was huddled, mumbling, on the edge of the bed – wearing Wellingtons, jeans and several sweaters. Sherwood and Strover were seated side by side on chairs in front of her. 'I got the impression of an interrogation and I said: "What are you doing to her? You are screwing up her mind and you will drive her into a mental home." ' She added that Sherwood then poked at her with a Bible.

It was an interrogation and during the course of it, according to Sherwood, Beatrix complained of being 'vexed with evil spirits'. He claimed that she asked for them to be cast out and that, although he had never made a study of exorcism, he decided to perform a ceremony.

He and Strover took her to the church where they prayed and then, when they returned to the flat, he was convinced that he saw a devil hovering over Beatrix.

He was clutching a Bible in court as he continued with his evidence: 'I cannot describe it to you. I cannot describe what an evil spirit looks like. This was my first experience – I had never actually seen a demon myself. My own strength seemed to have been taken over. I became filled with hatred for this evil spirit. I didn't have any feeling of violence to Beatrix in any way . . . thinking back, I can only say I completely lost control. I was wrestling with the devil within her and calling out for his name. I remember him telling me his name. It was Jack the Ripper. The voice was not hers. It was a deeper voice. I wasn't hallucinating in any way. It was a different being to me. It was against the devil that my attack was directed. I believe he went out of her. I am not exactly conscious of what I did but I know I was forcing the devil out through pockets of air, trying to push down. And every time I did, he became manifest and lingered in her face . . .'

Strover said that the exorcism attempt began with Sherwood hitting Beatrix: 'She was thrown on the bed. I told him to hold her legs and started hitting her in the stomach. I seemed to go berserk and just carried on. I did not believe that exorcising a person could hurt them but just the spirit would be cast out. I trusted John to know what to do.'

There were two thirty-minute sessions in which they punched, kicked and stamped on her. During those sessions they claimed another spirit identified itself as that of Judas Iscariot.

Strover added: 'I think I was using quite a lot of force. At the end I was exhausted. I was conscious that what we were doing could hurt her but, as we were dealing with the supernatural, I thought it would be in God's hands.'

Eventually Beatrix seemed calm and the two of them knelt beside her for a while in prayer – before realising that she was dead. The pathologist reported that she had multiple fractures of the rib-cage and that her liver had been split. Death had been caused by haemorrhage.

Initially, Sherwood refused to recognise the finality of her death. He said in court: 'I believed she could be resuscitated. We prayed that the Lord would bring her back to life. I read an account of Elijah bringing back to life a boy by laying on him. I got a blanket and lay on Beatrix and breathed into her mouth and tried to give her artificial respiration. It didn't seem to work and we prayed again as in the case of Lazarus that Jesus Christ would raise her up.' In his view, her body had been injured 'by the great force of devils leaving her'.

They maintained a twenty-four hour vigil by her body and only then, feeling their prayers were not being answered, did they go to the police. They were accused of murder, but after a defence plea, the charge was changed to manslaughter. For the defence, Mr Tudor Price said: 'It is not alleged they intended to kill her but it was the sad result of their misguided and unlawful act that brought about her death.'

In his summing-up the judge, Mr Justice Smith said: 'No one has questioned the defendants' state of mind. There is no question of mental illness.' He warned members of the jury against making any decision based on their personal views about exorcism and added: 'It does not matter what I or you think about exorcism but it is clear that the defendants believe in exorcism of evil spirits and that it is possible to drive evil spirits out of the body. Whether this belief is good, bad or rubbish, they sincerely believe it is the case.'

The verdict was guilty and the judge told the two men: 'I say straight away I must send you to prison. It is a painful duty because, unusually for these courts, you are upright Christian men acting, I am satisfied, out of misguided motives and not acting maliciously. But there must be some punishment. A life has been taken by brutal and sustained violence.'

Then, before hearing the length of the sentence, Sherwood took the opportunity to deliver a brief sermon from the dock: 'With the increase of evil in the world, the deliverance from evil through exorcism is becoming more and more important. And as time goes on we should consider that Jesus Christ has victory over the devil and realise what a formidable foe the evil one can be. Far being it from my intention that this should ever happen again. Jesus Christ came to this world to save sinners, of which I am the chief one.'

The hearing had lasted three days. The sentence: three years in prison.

The Reverend Neil-Smith told me afterwards: 'In the Church of England an exorcist should have at least a year's training by another priest before embarking on a ritual of exorcism. It is of paramount importance, also, to have the ability to discern between mental illness and spiritual torment in a person. These young men had never done an exorcism before. They went in where many wiser men would fear to tread.'

10 Controversy within the churches

Exorcisms which have gone disastrously wrong have hardened the attitudes of religious leaders who would like to ban all attempts to 'cast out demons'. Many prominent clerics today consider themselves too enlightened to accept the possibility of possession. They endorse the view expressed by Dr Sandy Robertson: 'I baulk at the idea that there is a disembodied entity which can enter people. For most people ideas such as possession and witchcraft are obvious nonsense but for some suggestible people they seem to provide a ready explanation for conflicts and turmoil which really arise within themselves. These ideas can only add an element of superstitious fear to an already troubled mind.' This plunges them into conflict with others of equal eminence who insist that humans can be invaded by alien spirits and that invaluable work is being done by exorcists.

The Church of England is in great confusion on this issue. Its bishops are bitterly divided and are therefore failing, as a body, to give any cohesive guidance. The muddle is increased by the fact that contradictory stances have been taken by successive Archbishops of Canterbury.

Advocates of exorcism felt that an important principle was being established when the Bishop of Exeter's Commission made this recommendation: 'It is much to be desired that every diocesan bishop should appoint a priest as diocesan exorcist and that in each province centres of training should be established, if possible, in collaboration with our Roman Catholic brethren.'

It had been planned that the findings of this seven-person commission, which started its studies in 1963, would provide the official guidelines on exorcism in the Church of England.

Yet in 1975, only three years after its findings were published, the present Archbishop of Canterbury – Dr Robert Runcie, who was then Bishop of St Albans – made this announcement: 'I have written to all my rural deans saying that I don't give permission for clergy to conduct exorcisms and any questions surrounding exorcisms have to be referred to me.

'I don't believe that exorcism is necessary because we do not need special forms of prayer and ministry to cope with little spirits that might be floating around.'

Dr Runcie was one of the sixty-five theologians and academics who had written to the Archbishops of Canterbury and York to urge that exorcism should not be officially recognised by the Church. Such recognition, in his view, would mean going back to 'our intellectual cradle'.

At that time he had an adviser called Dom Robert Petitpierre, a Benedictine monk, whom, he said, he could call in to explain the dangers to vicars wanting to conduct exorcisms. That struck me as puzzling for it was Dom Robert – regarded as one of the most experienced exorcists in Britain – who edited the findings of the Bishop of Exeter's Commission. And he had already told me: 'Wonderful results can be achieved by casting-out ceremonies for people's minds *are* sometimes infiltrated by non-human entities.' I have double-checked with Dom Robert. His opinion has not changed. So what, in these circumstances, is the role of an expert adviser? Is it intended that he should suppress his own views, however valid they may be, in deference to those preferred by a bishop? That would hardly savour of a determined bid to establish the truth about exorcism – or to spread a greater understanding of such truth.

Maybe Dr Runcie considers himself to be so sophisticated in his beliefs that he would like to turn back the clock to 1603 when, for a while, exorcism was outlawed by the Church of England. His thinking is certainly out-of-line with that of earlier Archbishops of Canterbury.

The Most Reverend Michael Ramsey said: 'I believe there is genuine demonic possession and a genuine exorcism, but the genuine element is probably in the minority. If there is an immense craze on the subject, it is a sign of spiritual immaturity.' He was stressing the need for caution, recognising that many reports of possession are based on errors or fabrications, but he was also proclaiming, unequivocally, his support for exorcism.

His successor, Dr Donald Coggan, also gave public backing to the practice of exorcism. In April 1975, four months after becoming Archbishop, he said: 'If you read the New Testament, you will find that Jesus exercised a liberating ministry. When a man came under the power of evil, He released him and set him free. Our task is continuing that work – the liberation from bondage to evil into fullness of life. That is the work of the Church. This has been the task of the Church down the years. It is a difficult task and the forces of evil are very great.

'I do not see exorcism as something set off against and in opposition to medicine. Far from it. I think there are many cases where the more rash exorcists have by-passed the work of psychiatrists and some of the cases where exorcism has been applied should not have occurred at all. They should have been referred to a psychiatrist. But there is no doubt that there are many cases of men and women so within the grip of the power of evil that they need the aid of the Christian church, working in collaboration with the forces of medicine, to deliver the person so oppressed.'

By this time the Church of England had issued fresh guidelines as a result of the Yorkshire tragedy involving Michael Taylor:

1) Exorcism should be done in collaboration with the resources of medicine.
2) In the context of prayer and sacrament.
3) With the minimum of publicity.
4) By an experienced person authorised by the Diocesan Bishop.
5) With continuing pastoral care.

Dr Coggan then made a direct reference to the Taylor case: 'Obviously there was a very grave mishandling of that poor creature and the Bishop of Wakefield indicated quite clearly that the Church of England and Methodist clergymen mishandled the thing very badly. The best things when they go wrong are a pretty awful mess so we should not condemn the ministry of liberation (exorcism) because there has been a bad case of it in the Diocese of Wakefield.'

We can draw one deduction from the views of successive Archbishops of Canterbury: the Church of England is riding a seesaw on the subject of exorcism. There is a lack of consistency in the authority which its laity – and, indeed, its priests – should expect to flow from the Palace at Lambeth. In fact, the Church is floundering on this aspect of its spiritual responsibilities and the confusion is being compounded by disagreement amongst the bishops.

The late Right Reverend David Brown, the Bishop of Guildford, advised his clergy not to 'dabble in exorcism'. In his diocesan leaflet of August 1981 he wrote:

> Many people today are interested in those strange elements in human nature often described as the psychic and the paranormal. Sometimes these phenomena are given a religious character and occasionally said to be gifts of the Holy Spirit. Some even claim to recognise the activity of evil spirits and to deliver those who, they say, are demon-possessed from their power.
>
> I do not deny that people are sometimes influenced by outside pressures, such as mass hysteria or environment, but I do not myself find it helpful to interpret the influence of evil in the personal form that belief in evil spirits suggests.

Some people might feel that the Bishop was impugning the guidance given repeatedly by Christ. In Mark 16 He is quoted as saying: 'These signs will accompany those who believe – In my name they will drive out demons.'

The Bishop anticipated such criticism, because he continued: 'In His human life He was subject to the limitations of human existence and the extent of His knowledge was that of a man of His own time.'

So what does that suggest? That Christ had only a shallow understanding of things spiritual? That His views should be discounted as nonsense?

What impact did the findings of the Bishop of Exeter's Commission have in the Diocese of Exeter?

A new bishop had been appointed by 1981 when I tried to contact the diocesan exorcist. There was not one and I was assured that, despite the recommendation I have quoted, there never had been one. The bishop's spokesman, Prebendary John Parkinson, said that there were priests 'who feel capable of handling this sort of thing' and that, if necessary, the bishop would ask them to see people seeking help. These priests were required to operate with great discretion to avoid becoming 'inundated by cranks'.

How many Church of England exorcisms had been sanctioned in the diocese during the previous twelve months?

'I don't know,' he replied. 'And it would be impossible for me to find out.' That struck me as a curious reply, for I would have expected that a record would have been kept of the number of officially-sanctioned exorcisms. Prebendary Parkinson could confirm, however, that 'the figure would have been very low'.

He seemed genuinely surprised when I explained to him that, because of a belief that no Church of England exorcisms were conducted in the diocese, Anglicans were turning for help to other faiths.

This occurs throughout the UK. And the fact that many Anglican churchgoers are reluctant to confide some of their spiritual fears to vicars – possibly because of the well-publicised pronouncements of men at the helm – is surely an indictment of the modern Church of England.

Jews and Moslems also seek help in other faiths because nearly all their own religious leaders, particularly in Western countries, refuse to accept the concept of possession. Yet their own faiths have a long heritage of elaborate beliefs.

Demons, or *djinn*, were created out of smokeless fire long before the first man, according to Islamic tradition, and they will still be here when all humans have died. They are usually invisible, although they can appear as animals, and they can take possession of whole communities as well as of invidivuals. Islamic leaders in Britain have veered away from these old ideas. They dismiss *djinn*-possession as mythology.

Psychologist Professor Zaki Badawi, Director of the Islamic Cultural Centre in London, told me: 'Rituals still being conducted by Moslems in more primitive parts of the world are quite extraordinary and some are extremely dangerous. There are certain exorcists who feel that *djinn* must be driven away by punishment, and that the best way to inflict such punishment is to beat the people said to be possessed or to lock them in a dark room. I know of cases in which victims – people who were ill, mentally or physically, rather than possessed – have been killed by this sort of treatment and I would prohibit all exorcisms.'

One young Egyptian child with a history of convulsions was put into a pan of boiling water to be cleared of an 'evil spirit' – and died of burns.

In Britain, says Professor Badawi, there is a procedure for helping those who consider themselves to be possessed. An *iman* holds their hands and recites two Surahs from the Koran: 'In the Name of God, the Most Gracious, the Dispenser of Grace . . . I seek refuge with the Sustainer of the rising dawn, from the evil of aught that He has created and from the evil of all human beings bent on occult endeavours, and from the evil of the envious when he envies . . . I seek refuge with the Sustainer of men, the Sovereign of men, the God of men, from the evil of the whispering elusive tempter who whispers in the hearts of men, from all invisible forces as well as men.'

And if a man should then persist in the conviction that he is possessed?

Professor Badawi shrugged. 'Then it might be necessary for him to see a psychiatrist.'

Jewish belief in demons, or *dybbukim*, is enshrined in the cabbala – the theosophy claimed to have been passed on through the patriarchs and prophets since the creation of the first man – in which they are regarded as the incarnation of all human vices. Yet, curiously, the original *dybbukim*, like the *djinn*, were supposedly here before the first man. Their prince was Samael, the serpent spirit which seduced Eve.

The Hebrew word *dybbuk* means 'attachment' and is used as an abbreviation of the phrase *dybbuck m'ruach raa* – 'attachment of an evil spirit'. The tradition of casting out *dybbukim* stretches back long before the days of Christ. An early ritual was described by the Jewish historian Josephus, who was born in

Jerusalem in the first year of the reign of Caligula:

> I have seen a certain man of my own country, whose name was Eleazar, releasing people that were demoniacal, in the presence of Vespasian and his sons and his captains and the whole multitude of soldiers. The manner of the cure was this: He put a ring that had a root of one of those sorts mentioned by Solomon to the nostrils of the demoniac, after which he drew the demon through his nostrils; and when the man fell down, immediately he abjured him to return into him no more, still making mention of Solomon, and reciting the incantations he composed . . .

Then Elezear, who was renowned as a mystic, gave a calculated display of showmanship: 'He sat a little way off a cup or a basin full of water and commanded the demon, as he went out of the man, to overturn it, and thereby let the spectators know that he had left the man.'

By the end of the twelfth century the concept of *dybbuck*-possession started to merge with that of *gilgul* – the transmigration of souls – which led to the conviction that the living could be entered by the restless dead. Specialist Masters of the Divine Name, the Baal Shem, later emerged to counter these attacks. Most of them also used beatings as a form of exorcism.

A graphic eyewitness account of a Jewish exorcism was provided by a Polish Jew, Jacob Fromer, in an autobiography* published in 1812. A girl was said to have become possessed by the spirit of a learned man who, after years of depravity and drunkenness, had committed suicide by drowning. Fromer wrote:

> The wide and spacious room where the girl had been brought and seated on a chair in the middle was filled with the serried ranks of the crowd. I had a good place from which I could see and hear everything. She sat down, languid and exhausted, with haggard, fearful eyes, and from time to time lamented, begging to be taken back to the house because she was afraid

* Translated by D. Idderson and quoted by Professor T. K. Oesterreich in *Possession, Demoniacal and Other*, published by Paul, Trench and Tauber in 1930.

> of the wonder-rabbi. Her voice, weak and beseeching, inspired sympathy and compassion.

Fromer and other onlookers were astounded when the girl suddenly sprang up and, making a great effort to remain standing, shouted: *'Silentium strictissimum!'*

> I could not believe my ears. It was a real man's voice, harsh and rough, and the onlookers affirmed that it was exactly the voice of the *meshoummed,* the baptised man. Not one of us knew the meaning of these words. We only knew that it was a strange language which the sick woman understood as little as ourselves.
>
> 'Ladies and gentlemen,' continued she . . . Then she pronounced a long, confused discourse with High German turns of phrase of which I understood only that it greeted a festive gathering and wished to draw attention to the meaning of the feast. She broke off in the middle of this speech and burst into a frightful laugh which made us shudder to the marrow. I was as if thunderstruck.

Then the rabbi commanded the possessing entity to identify itself and he became angry when the girl, softly and faintly, replied, 'Esther.' She was to be silent, he said, because he was addressing the *dybbuck.* He threatened that he would beat her with a *loulaf* (palm frond) if the *dybbuck* refused to reply and then the girl, once again, seemed to speak with the harsh voice of a man: 'Do not strike me . . . I will reply.' It then identified itself and begged not to be expelled but soon its attitude changed. It started laughing and it taunted the rabbi with a 'coarse insult'. Fromer wrote:

> The rabbi changed colour and shook with rage and excitement. He had never yet encountered such impudence. But he recovered his self-control rapidly seized the *loulaf* and struck the girl violently in the face with it. Then an incredible thing happened; the girl (who was being held) had freed her hands with lightning speed and before anyone could prevent her she dealt the rabbi two resounding blows on the ears.
>
> A panic followed. The frightened crowd uttered cries and

oaths, storming and weeping with excitement. Never had the like been seen. Nevertheless, strong arms had seized the sick girl, the rabbi struck her so furiously with the *loulaf* that her face streamed with blood; she collapsed with a terrible cry and became unconscious.

At this moment a noise was heard at the window as if it had been struck by a small stone. Everyone rushed towards it and discovered in one pane a hole the size of a pea, through which aperture the spirit had fled. The girl was carried out.

After this scene I was as if transformed. I had come there as an unbeliever, an atheist, ostensibly to study on-the-spot superstition, religious dementia. The experience of an hour had sufficed to overthrow like a house of cards the independent ideas which I had acquired by years of study, trial and struggles. In vain I told myself a thousand times that the girl was ill, that she had been in touch with the dead man in his lifetime and might have imitated his voice and manner of speech. In vain I asserted that the rabbi had executed an illusion with involuntary comic effect. Before me were thousands of men, older, more experienced, wiser than I. They all believed in the existence of the *dybbuck*, they had seen the spirit come out, they had heard the impact on the window and seen the hole in the pane . . .

Now that I am committing these thoughts to writing I can, if I wish, call these men fools. What is there to prevent me? I am sitting alone in my room, have paper and pen and can think and write what I please. But at that moment I found myself like a single and tiny intelligence amongst thousands of stronger ones which weighed me down, absorbed me and carried me away.

My position today, more than 150 years later, mirrors that of Fromer. I, too, am alone in my room with paper and pen. I, too, can write what I please. Although I am not an atheist, I also approached the subject of exorcism with cautious scepticism. Much of that scepticism, like Fromer's, has been stripped away by the evidence. I am convinced that there is a very deep need for the services of responsible exorcists.

Many modern Jews like Fromer are certainly prepared to recognise the possibility of possession but Rabbi Dr Harry Rabinowicz emphasises that there is now no Jewish exorcism in Britain. People who consider themselves to be possessed are usually given an amulet and a scroll bearing sacred words. 'And the need for that sort of help is extremely rare,' said Dr Rabinowicz. 'I have encountered only one or two cases in twenty years.'

Could that be because most Jews, like most Moslems, know the attitude of their hierarchy and, not wishing to risk being ridiculed, take such spiritual anxieties to men in other faiths?

A Jewish businessman is amongst those who has been salvaged by a priest in the Church of England. He was convinced at first that he had been working too hard, that exhaustion was driving him towards a nervous breakdown. He had been a successful entrepreneur but he could no longer cope with his responsibilities and, in his own words, he became 'mentally paralysed'.

It did not occur to him that his problems could have some psychic origin until one evening when he returned to his flat. As he stepped into the drawingroom an invisible force lifted him off the floor and flung him hard to the far side of the room. Then he recognised – or he *thought* he recognised – the cause of his trouble. The flat was haunted. Something was infesting the place – devil . . . demon . . . *dybbuck*. He decided that the responsibility lay with the estate agents. He gave them an ultimatum: either they resolve the matter quickly or he would let other tenants know there was dangerous evil in the building.

The agents anxiously sought the help of Father Ian Hazlewood who exorcised and blessed the flat principally to satisfy the man, although he was not at all convinced that the root of the problem was there. There was an evil spirit but Hazlewood felt it was inside the man and so he suggested that the demoniac should also be exorcised.

The possessed lay on the chancel floor and Father Hazlewood sprinkled him with holy water. An alien spirit was then cast out. The man was able to return home without fear and resume work with confident efficiency.

The Church of Scotland also frowns on exorcism. Its Knoxian General Assembly has declared: 'Exorcism does more harm than good. There is no place for it in the Church of Scotland.'

Baptist and Methodist ministers have complete freedom to make their own decisions about the value of exorcism. However, there are guidelines. One of the key ones within Methodism reads:

> There should be a thorough pastoral investigation of the case including, save in totally exceptional circumstances, close and continuing collaboration with suitable persons qualified in medicine, psychology and the social services, including the appropriate referral of the person seeking help. The form of any service of healing for those believed or believing themselves to be possessed should be considered in consultation with the ministerial staff of the circuit (or, in one-minister circuits, with those whom the Chairman of the District suggests). Such a service should not be carried out when a person is in a highly excited state. It should not be unnecessarily prolonged. Publicity must be kept to a minimum.

The way Methodist ministers are free to make their own basic decisions was emphasised in a Statement on Exorcism which was adopted by the Methodist Conference in 1976. It says:

> Three differing views currently held by Christians are:
> 1) The process of exorcism involves the casting out of an objective power of evil which has gained possession of a person. This view includes the conviction that the authority to exorcise has been given to the Church as one of the ways in which Christ's Ministry is continued in the world. Some who hold this view believe in the ontological reality of evil spirits; others prefer to speak of people as being overpowered by a personal force of evil.
> 2) The process of exorcism is a necessary or at least an effective psychological means of reassuring those who believe themselves to be possessed. In this case, performing the rite of exorcism according to the New Testament pattern does not

involve the minister in accepting for himself the ontological reality of the spirits which are removed, although he accepts their psychological reality for the person who believes himself to be possessed.

3) A belief in demons is explicable sociologically and psychologically. It is undeniable that there are people who claim to believe in demons, but – since demons do not exist – it is their belief with which we should deal, not demons. In this case exorcism would be inappropriate, since what is to be dealt with is false belief. To pretend to accept a situation which is false is not a means of bringing people to the truth. Those who take this view stress that the normal ministry of words and sacraments, together with appropriate pastoral care, can deal with these situations. Fears and anxieties can be dealt with by the assurance of the presence and love of Christ. On this basis, the wholeness which God wills for all people can be discovered and the necessity of exorcism is excluded.

Only the first of these views would be endorsed by the Roman Catholic Church. It is unswerving in the conviction that possession is an undeniable reality – that alien spirits can be countered by ritual blessings and by elaborate ceremonies of exorcism.

The Church's belief in the Devil as an entity was expressed in 1972 by Pope Paul VI: 'We know that this dark and disturbing spirit really exists and that he still acts with treacherous cunning.'

Current views were summed up for me by the Jesuit, Father John Tracy: 'We have come a long way from the superstitious notions of the Middle Ages. At one time, for example, it was believed, quite wrongly, that diabolical possession was invariably Divine punishment on a grievous sinner. However, we know that there are demons. That is made perfectly clear in Sacred Scripture which is part of the whole Judaeo-Christian heritage. And these demons are capable of possessing humans. Of that, there is no doubt.'

The Roman Catholic rite for combatting them has changed through the years. At one time the exorcist was permitted to use prayers and commands which he personally considered most suitable. Now he must not deviate from the prescribed pattern.

The Vatican-approved Rules state:

> He should not believe too readily that a person is possessed by an evil spirit; but he ought to ascertain the signs by which a person possessed can be distinguished from one who is suffering from some illness, especially one of a psychological nature.
>
> Signs of possession may be the following – ability to speak with some facility in a strange tongue or to understand it when spoken by another; the faculty of divulging future or hidden events; display of powers which are beyond the subject's age and natural condition; and various other indications which, when taken together as a whole, build up the evidence.

The Roman Catholic priest should go to confession before conducting an exorcism and, in addition to offering prayers for help, he should say the Litany of the Saints. Any relics of the saints which might be available should be applied to the breast or head of the demoniac who should be bound if there is any danger of violence.

The Rules add: 'One will see to it that these sacred objects are not treated improperly or that no injury is done them by the evil spirit. However, one should not hold the holy Eucharist over the head of the person or in any way apply it to his body, owing to the danger of desecration.'

Before addressing himself directly to the demon, the priest must continue praying: 'God, whose nature is ever merciful and forgiving, accept our prayer that this servant of yours, bound by the fetters of sin, may be pardoned by your loving kindness . . .'

Although the form of rite has been up-dated, the language of the special prayers and commands remains colourfully archaic. This prayer goes on:

> Holy Lord, almighty Father, everlasting God and Father of our Lord Jesus Christ, who once and for all consigned that fallen and apostate tyrant to the flames of hell, who sent your

> only-begotten Son into the world to crush that roaring lion; hasten to our call for help and snatch from ruination and from the clutches of the noonday devil this human being made in your image and likeness. Strike terror, Lord, into the beast now laying waste your vineyard. Fill your servants with courage to fight manfully against that reprobate dragon, lest he despise those who put their trust in you . . .

Then follow readings from the Holy Gospels and more prayers before it is time to cast out the demon:

> I adjure you, ancient serpent, by the judge of the living and the dead, by your Creator, by the Creator of the whole universe, by Him who has the power to consign you to hell, to depart forthwith in fear, along with your savage minions, from this servant of God . . . may the trembling that afflicts this human frame, the fear that afflicts this image of God, descend on you . . . do not think of despising my command because you know me to be a great sinner. It is God Himself who commands you; the majestic Christ who commands you . . . begone from this man (woman) who is His creature . . . the longer you delay the heavier your punishment shall be; for it is not men you are contemning, but rather Him who rules the living and the dead, who is coming to judge both the living and the dead and the world by fire . . .

Priests are instructed to be on guard against 'the arts and subterfuges which the evil spirits are wont to use in deceiving the exorcist'.

The Rules say:

> Often-times they give deceptive answers and make it difficult to understand them, so that the exorcist might tire and give up, or so it might appear that the afflicted one is in no wise possessed by the devil.
>
> Once in a while, after they are already recognised, they conceal themselves and leave the body practically free from every molestation, so that the victim believes himself completely delivered . . .
>
> Sometimes the devil will leave the possessed person in

peace and even allow him to receive the holy Eucharist, to make it appear that he has departed. In fact, the arts and frauds of the evil one for deceiving a man are innumerable. For this reason the exorcist must be on his guard not to fall into this trap . . .

The exorcist must not digress into senseless prattle, not ask superfluous questions or such as are prompted by curiosity, particularly if they pertain to future and hidden matters, all of which have nothing to do with his office. Instead, he will bid the unclean spirit keep silence and answer only when asked. Neither ought he to give any credence to the devil if the latter maintains that he is the spirit of some saint or of a deceased party . . .

Exorcisms end with this prayer:

Almighty God, we beg you to keep the evil spirit from further molesting this servant of yours, and to keep him far away, never to return. At your command, O Lord, may the goodness and peace of our Lord Jesus Christ, our Redeemer, take possession of this person. May we no longer fear any evil since the Lord is with us; who lives and reigns with you, in the unity of the Holy Spirit, God, forever and ever. Amen.

There is also a special rite for the cleansing of a locality or an entire community believed to be polluted by spiritual evil. This is known as Exorcism of Satan and the Fallen Angels, and it starts with a prayer to St Michael the Archangel:

Defend us in the battle against principalities and powers, against the rulers of the world of darkness and the spirit of wickedness in high places . . . entreat the Lord of peace to cast Satan down under our feet, so as to keep him from further holding man captive . . .carry our prayers up to God's throne, that the mercy of the Lord may quickly come and lay hold of the beast, the serpent of old, Satan and his demons, casting him in chains into the abyss, so that he can no longer seduce the nations . . .

Later come commands of dismissal to the 'accursed dragon

and every diabolical legion' – followed by a prayer to God: 'We humbly entreat your glorious majesty to deliver us by your might from every influence of the accursed spirits, from their every evil snare and deception, and to keep us from all harm.'

The area is then sprinkled with holy water.

11 Is the Bible wrong about exorcism and demons?

'Our fight is not against human foes, but against cosmic powers, against the authorities and potentates of this dark world, against the superhuman forces of evil in the heavens.'

That message was given by the Apostle Paul in his letter to the Ephesians (Chapter 6, Verse 12). The Archbishop of Canterbury, Dr Runcie, appeared to be trying to cut those 'authorities and potentates' down to size when he referred to 'little spirits that might be floating around'. In his denunciation of exorcism, Dr Runcie implied that Paul was a product of our 'intellectual cradle'. Does the Archbishop really believe that, in a strictly intellectual sense, men like Moses and, indeed, Christ Himself hardly progressed out of infancy? Should their guidance be seen as infantile and therefore suspect?

Similar questions might well be posed over the attitudes to Christ of the late Bishop Brown of Guildford, who said: 'In His human life He was subject to the limitations of human existence and the extent of His knowledge was that of a man of His own time.'

He also offered one of the standard anti-exorcism arguments: 'Some would say that our Lord cast out demons and that His ministers should do the same. This can be a real difficulty . . . medical science, including psychology and the study of mental disorders, has greatly advanced since His time and it is not always appropriate to use His language.'

Medical science has sometimes also advanced in the *wrong* direction and has been forced to retreat. This is exemplified in the work pioneered by the Nobel Prize-winner Egas Moniz in the field of pre-frontal leucotomy, which was lauded as the wonder method for alleviating various forms of mental orders. Before the devastating side-effects were fully estimated, it had been performed on thousands of patients.

The Bishop was right to have respect for medical science but medical scientists – together with psychiatrists and psychologists – are fallible. Even in the days of Christ, conditions other than demonosis were being diagnosed. In Matthew 4, Verse 24, we find this line: 'People brought to Him all who were sick with various diseases, those suffering severe pain, the demon-possessed, the epileptics and paralytics and He healed them . . .'

Christ and His contemporaries, unlike some of our modern evangelists, were not prepared to ascribe all ailments or afflictions to the work of demons.

The Church of England is in danger of veering off course, of becoming too 'enlightened' to accept fundamental truths.

* * *
* * *

A whirlpool of jealousies and controversies exists within faiths and between faiths. Even among those priests firmly dedicated to the Ministry of Deliverance, there is often antagonism, sometimes hardly veiled, for others who do not agree with them on certain aspects of theology. Father Wheaton is a Liberal Catholic, and cases are occasionally referred to him by a priest in the Church of England. That may seem sensible for the prime object is to help people in distress or danger and he has a great deal of success in this particular ministry. Mark 9, Verses 38 and 39, emphasises that theological disagreements and denominational demarcations should not hinder the work of God:

> John said to Him, 'Master, we saw a man driving out devils in your name and, as he was not one of us, we tried to stop him.' Jesus said, 'Do not stop him; no one who does a work of divine power in my name will be able the next moment to speak evil

of me. For he who is not against us is on our side.'

* * *

* * *

Many of the more 'trendy' people in the churches find difficulty in accepting that any spirit, whether baleful or benevolent, can assume an apparently solid and indentifiable form. Some cultivate scepticism as a form of protection. They half-believe that these accounts may be authentic but, finding that possibility too disturbing, they deliberately pull down a shutter. Yet does not the after-death appearance of a spirit – that of Jesus Christ – provide a cornerstone for their faith?

Father Arnold Clare elaborates: 'Those visitations of Christ did not involve ordinary flesh-and-blood. His spirit – like those of some demons and dead humans – was using elemental forces in order to become manifest. He could have assumed any shape but, determined to be recognised, he adopted the human form with which people were familiar.'

The Reverend George Tarleton replies: 'Jesus did live again as a real man after his death. He was solid flesh-and-blood – exactly as he'd been at the time of the crucifixion – and it's outrageous to suggest he was some kind of apparition.'

Tarleton points to the description, in Luke 24, verses 36 to 43, of Jesus appearing to his disciples:

> As they were talking about all this, there he was, standing among them. Startled and terrified, they thought they were seeing a ghost. But he said, 'Why are you so disturbed? Why do questionings arise in your minds? Look at my hands and feet. It is I myself. Touch me and see; no ghost has flesh and bones as you can see that I have.' They were still unconvinced, still wondering, for it seemed too good to be true. So he asked them, 'Have you anything here to eat?' They offered him a piece of fish they had cooked, which he took and ate before their eyes.

Tarleton adds: 'That passage cannot be misunderstood. It gives the clearest possible confirmation that Jesus returned as a flesh-and-blood man after the crucifixion.'

Yet other passages in the Bible indicate that Christ almost certainly was not *exactly* as he had been before his physical death.

St John describes how Mary Magdala, standing outside the empty tomb, 'saw Jesus standing there, but did not recognise him'. She thought, in fact, that he was the gardener and asked him if he had removed the body of Christ. So she was close enough to speak to him and yet did not recognise him until he replied. Does this not suggest he did not look *quite* the same?

St Mark describes what happened next: 'She went and carried the news to his mourning and sorrowful followers, but when they were told that he was alive and that she had seen him they did not believe it.'

They found it easier to assume, in other words, that she was lying or had suffered an hallucination.

Other testimonies brought a similar response. Mark continues: 'Later he appeared in a different guise to two of them as they were walking, on their way into the country. These also went and took the news to the others, but again no one believed them.'

The disciple Thomas, of course, was the classic disbeliever. He had not been present when Christ appeared to the other disciples in their locked room and he certainly was not going to take their word: 'Unless I see the mark of the nails on his hands, unless I put my finger into the place where the nails were, and my hand into his side, I will not believe it.'

Thomas was convinced, according to the Bible, when Christ again appeared within a locked room. And the mechanics of that appearance, like the first one in the room, prompts another question: real flesh-and-blood coming through a locked door or possibly even through a wall?

It is far more likely, surely, that the spirit of Christ was using powers similar to those employed by the demons which threatened Myers and Father Clare. There is also a similarity between his prime purpose and that of the demons. He wanted people to accept him fully into their hearts and minds – to be filled, in fact, with his spirit.

On the subject of possession, Roman Catholicism is the only

mainstream religion in Britain which is not riddled with doubting Thomases. All Catholic priests are frontline soldiers in the battle against disturbing psychic forces – rather than being little more than surpliced social workers – and they are all expected to perform ceremonies of spiritual cleansing. Most of these ceremonies take the form of a blessing. The Rules relating to exorcism are extremely rigid. This was emphasised by Father Brian Reeves of the Church of the Blessed Sacrament in Exeter: 'I am certainly not qualified to perform an exorcism, although I have been asked to do so several times, and the most I would do would be to bless a building or a person. However, the power of such a blessing, invoking the love of Jesus Christ, should never be underestimated.'

At their rented home in Exeter, four university students experienced the effectiveness of that power, after being frightened for months by an 'invisible ghost'. The property was owned by a woman who had lived in it for years, before moving into a new house nearby, and they complained to her that the front door was often flung open, despite having been locked, and was then slammed hard. The slamming noise would always be followed by the sound of heavy footsteps across the hall and up the stairs.

'The landlady is a woman I know well,' said Father Reeves. 'She and her husband had been aware of this phenomenon regularly during their years in the house but had not mentioned it to the students. It had not worried her but now, because it was causing distress, she wanted it cleared.'

A few days later the students were grouped around him as he sprinkled holy water through the house and gave the formal blessing: 'Blessed are you, Lord God, King of all creation: through your goodness you have given this house to be a home for your children [he named each of the students]. Let your peace remain with them always. Let all who come here to their life find generosity, tranquillity and happiness; may they depart enriched by the joy of Christian living. Lord, may this water, blessed in your name, be a sign of your protection for those who live here, for their home and for all things in it. Protect them from all harm, give them your peace and remain with them now and always. We ask this blessing through Christ our Lord. Amen.'

The slamming door and phantom footsteps ceased.

The simplicity of that blessing contrasts starkly with the evocative incantations used in Catholic exorcisms. The roaring lion and the noonday devil and the reprobate dragon . . . do they need to be identified so specifically? Or are many of the words and phrases, which were probably once accepted literally, now little more than a form of religious window-dressing?

Confrontations with demons are events of high drama. I see little benefit in heightening an already highly-charged emotional atmosphere through slavish adherence to such repetitive ritual dramatics. A simpler style of ceremony, in which the supplications could be just as devoutly sincere, would be more appropriate.

One of the statutory prayers contains these requests: 'God, Creator and defender of the human race, who made man in your own image, look down in pity on this your servant [name], now in the toils of the unclean spirit, now caught up in the fearsome threats of man's ancient enemy, sworn foe of our race, who befuddles and stupefies the human mind, throws it into terror, overwhelms it with fear and panic. Repel, O Lord, the devil's power, break asunder his snares and traps, put the unholy tempter to flight . . . Graciously grant, O Lord, as we call on your holy name, that the evil spirit who hitherto terrorised us, may himself retreat in terror and defeat, so that this servant of yours may sincerely and steadfastly render you the service which is your due . . .'

Do Catholic exorcists believe that the Almighty needs to have any possessing entity described in such repetitive detail? They cannot argue that the information needs to be given as a form of background briefing – to ensure that He fully appreciates the seriousness of the situation – for that would be to suggest a divine lack of understanding and intelligence. Nor would they claim that any sincere and justified supplication would be capriciously ignored if the phraseology were not considered satisfactory by Him.

Demoniacs are extremely vulnerable and should not be

subjected to additional pressures.

This criticism of the Catholic rite does not mean that, on the broad issue of exorcism, I am not in sympathy with the attitude of the Roman Catholic Church. My researches have persuaded me that many of the exorcisms performed on individuals in Britain, possibly the majority, are not really necessary. They do little good and, indeed, can cause varying degress of mental or emotional damage. Others certainly bring therapeutic benefits to victims of non-spiritual afflictions. A small percentage really do culminate in the casting-out of spiritual trespassers. Those trespassers would be allowed to flourish, so developing a greater potential for destruction, if it were not for the efforts of properly qualified exorcists.

This is why the current controversy about exorcism within the churches – and particularly the pressure for it to be banned – is immensely disturbing.

12 Is there a genuine need for exorcism?

Misguided attempts at exorcism have ended in tragedies. Have there been other tragedies which might have been averted by effective exorcism? Have spiritual maggots thrived in human minds, unrecognised and unchecked, until they were powerful enough to cause death?

Three-year-old Cassandra Wickenden of Birmingham perished in a mysterious fire at her home. An open verdict was recorded on her death in 1980. The ordeal described by her parents was comparable to that suffered, about the same time, by the family of little Bradley Burden in Bournemouth. The details also had chilling similarities with those portrayed in the film *The Shining* in which a seven-year-old girl has the ability to communicate with ghosts and to cause terrifying manifestations.

The coroner, Dr Richard Whittingdon, clashed with Cassandra's parents because they wanted an expert on extrasensory perception to be called as a witness. He ruled that ESP could have nothing to do with the case and added: 'I do not accept this as evidence in court.'

He had already heard from fire brigade officials and a detective that no cause could be found for the fire in the child's bedroom and he suggested that it might have been started by a cigarette burning in the next bedroom.

Cassandra's mother sobbed and shouted from the back of the court: 'Nobody had been up there. It did not start like that.'

Here we see a direct parallel with the frightening events which started at the Burdens' home in 1979 – when the candles suddenly became alight and when the bed mysteriously burst into flames.

Cassandra's father later claimed that his daughter 'had her ghost man and wanted to play with him'. He explained: 'She had been on about it and said she was going to go with him and be with him all the time. We put it down to a child's imagination.'

That opinion was soon to change when Wickenden saw the phantom man. 'I saw him moving around the room. The house was haunted. We had a Baptist minister in to exorcise it. But after a week or so Cassie realised that the man had not been there. She called him back so that she could play.'

The Burden home was also 're-polluted' after exorcism. That was why there were further ceremonies of exorcism, which were more powerful and effective. Is it possible that young Cassandra might have been saved from death if similar action had been taken at her home? Her father said, 'Cassie could move things off shelves out of reach. She would stand and watch something and the next thing we knew it would be on the floor without her touching it. She was hyperactive. She had very strong ESP and it was being examined by a psychiatrist.'

He and his wife claimed they first noticed strange happenings when Cassandra was about a year old and very advanced mentally for her age. 'If Cassie did not get attention, things would start happening. Once, when I smacked her on the legs for being naughty, a dining chair just flew across the room. A few days later, after I told her off, there was the most terrible banging on the ceiling and the whole house felt as if it was vibrating.'

Earlier, in the courtroom, Mrs Wickenden had shouted at the coroner: 'Why don't you believe us?'

The coroner's refusal to believe was hardly surprising. The concept of possession or possible possession strikes many people, including experts within the churches and the medical profession, as too bizarre for serious consideration. Yet the open verdict on Cassandra showed that no acceptable 'rational' explanation could be established for the cause of her death.

The possibility of other types of misery being alleviated by exorcism was raised by Peter Thompson of the Matthew Trust when he spoke of mental patients who are considered undiagnosable: 'Most of them are people who have committed out-of-character crimes while mentally-ill – or possibly while possessed by demons – but, because they cannot be diagnosed, the trigger that set them off hasn't been discovered. So they have to stay inside until the trigger is found.'

Some patients in this category have been released before psychiatrists have accurately identified that 'trigger'. The consequences can be horrendous. That was demonstrated in the case of Graham Young who was transformed from an unremarkable schoolboy into one of the most callous poisoners of this century – after having become obsessed by black magic.

Young was born in London in 1947. In 1962 he admitted that he had poisoned four people, including his father and stepmother. An Old Bailey judge sent him to Broadmoor and recommended that he should not be released for at least fifteen years. He was freed in February 1971. He resumed his career as a 'motiveless poisoner', this time at Hemel Hempstead, and in 1972 he appeared at St Albans Crown Court in connection with the poisoning of eight people, two of whom had died. The charges included murder and he was given a life sentence.

Should the authorities not question whether these later tragedies might have been averted if an attempt had been made to cleanse him through exorcism? Such a ceremony would have involved no risk and, in view of his background, it was surely worth considering.

His early 'unhealthy obsessions' were described by his sister, Winifred Young, in *Obsessive Poisoner* (published by Robert Hale):

> In the year before he was arrested for the first time he became interested in Black Magic. He once asked Sandra, a cousin, whether she was interested in the subject or had read anything about it but she told him she wasn't interested. Nevertheless, as was his way, he *insisted* upon talking about it and went on to describe how it involved saying the Lord's Prayer backwards, and hanging crucifixes upside down. He said he had met 'a chap' while visiting the library who was a member of a Black Magic circle in Willesden and who had told him a great deal about the work of a coven . . . Sandra and my Aunt Win went through his pockets in fact shortly before his first

> arrest and they discovered a plasticine figure lying alongside a couple of darning needles. The 'body' was rust-coloured with green legs. This obviously had something to do with his interest in Back Magic . . . As he grew older, too, he became more and more inclined to doodle. And what strange and weird doodles they were . . . devils' heads, skulls and cross-bones and a great string of incomprehensible letters . . .

His sister occasionally suggested remedies to lift him from his depressions: 'He shook his head. "No," he said, and I shall never forget his words, "Nothing like that can help. You see, there's a terrible coldness inside me." '

Coldness. That word is used often by people aware of real psychic evil. Was it a coincidence that it should overlap between people who are mentally sick and those who are attracted to black magic? Psychiatrists such as Dr Mackarness and Dr McAll confirm that an individual with an unbalanced mind, or a completely deranged mind, is likely to be intrigued by the darker side of the occult. And sane people drawn into its dangerous mysteries can eventually be tipped off balance. Which came first, the sickness or the attraction? Did one cause the other? Or, indeed, is there absolutely no link?

We do not know if Young was demon-possessed. We do know that he was just one of at least five 'rehabilitated' mental patients who went back into society and committed murder.

Medical science failed these patients. It also must take some blame for the fate of their subsequent victims. It is extraordinary that exorcism was not officially sanctioned – even on an experimental basis – for any one of these patients.

There was a chance that lives might have been saved. Certain priests claim that they have achieved good results by performing 'placebo exorcisms' – by going through the motions of driving out demons simply to bring psychosomatic relief. In the right circumstances it makes good sense.

There are those who believe themselves to be demon-plagued and who can feel resentfully frustrated if told repeatedly that they are wrong. They *know* they are right and the lack of recognition in others makes them feel alienated. That builds a barrier between them and their recovery. Occasionally it is advisable for a helper – priest or doctor – to go through the charade of believing. Dr Walter Franklin Prince, former research director of the American and Boston Societies for Psychical Research, has achieved successes with this technique. His paper, 'Two Cures for "Paranoia" by Experimental Appeals to Purported Obsessing Spirits', explained:

> That my acknowledgement that the imagined obsessions might be actual ones, my agreement that the patient might be right in his (or her) opinion, put him (or her) into a favourable state of mind, a state of satisfaction with the admission, in which my exhortations to the imagined spirits to cease their mischief could act as suggestions operating in the patient.

This follows the well-proven principle that your mind can make you sick or well, that habits of thought can make a measurable impact on mental or physical health, that people can be helped simply by being convinced that they are being helped.

Priests have a duty to attempt to help those who believe themselves to be spiritually troubled – even if the belief is based on a delusion.

* * *

* * *

One of the most startling cases of alleged mass possession was witnessed in 1634 at the Ursuline Convent in Loudun. Priests and nuns were said to have been galvanised into scandalous sexual activities by an evil psychic invasion. In *The Devils of Loudun* (published by Chatto and Windus) Aldous Huxley said:

> There is nothing, so far as I can see, self-contradictory in the idea of possession. The notion is not one to be ruled out *a priori* on the ground that it is a 'relic of ancient superstition'. It should be treated rather as a working hypothesis, which may be cautiously entertained in any case where other forms of explanation are found to be inadequate to the fact.

Another hypothesis which should be 'cautiously entertained' concerns the possible identity of non-human entities which are often described by priests as 'fragments of psychic evil'. Is it not possible that some of them may simply be 'misplaced spirits' – the earth-bound spirits of animals which have trespassed into human bodies? They could well create distress or even carnage, not because they are psychic evil but merely because they are in the wrong physical frame. A leopard, in itself, is not evil. But if the spirit of a dead leopard were to enter a suburban man and manipulate his behaviour . . . then we would certainly get the impression of truly appalling evil. The possessed man who barks like a dog or the woman who displays the characteristics of a reptile . . . is it not conceivable that they have been entered by the spirits of such creatures?

Maybe man is the only creature consciously aware of his own physical mortality but it would be ludicrous to deny that animals also have spirits. What happens to those spirits after death? Are they simply snuffed out? Or do they also move on to some higher plane?

St Paul broached this subject in his first letter to the Corinthians:

> You may ask, how are the dead raised? In what kind of body? How foolish! The seed you sow does not come to life unless it has first died; and what you sow is not the body that shall be, but a naked grain, perhaps of wheat, or of some other kind; and God clothes it with the body of His choice, each seed with its own particular body. All flesh is not the same flesh: there is flesh of men, flesh of beast, of birds and of fishes – all different . . . what is sown in the earth as a perishable thing is raised imperishable . . . sown as an animal body, it is raised as a spiritual body. If there is such a thing as an animal body, there is also a spiritual body.

Deaths which are violent or unexpectedly premature can result in human spirits being tethered to this world. Some of these spirits appear to be held by bonds of devotion, as in the case of Richard Johnson who was killed in a car accident. Others, like Bridget Pettigrew, are imprisoned by their earthly-life jealousies or hatreds. Pet owners agree that comparable emotions can be seen in animals. They can display deep love for people and places. They can also be possessive or can display violent dislikes.

So is it not feasible that animal spirits may also be earthbound?

The ordeal of the Burden family, according to the exorcists involved, was caused by the spirit of a drug addict. Similar ordeals might be traced to the spirits of dead creatures. Perhaps, even, to a poisoned rat or a fox killed by a speeding car.

Some spiritualists claim to have the help of animal spirit guides. Their claims should not be lightly dismissed. Nor should the possibility of possession by the non-human dead.

Today there is an increasing tendency for people to regard churches as places to be entered only for weddings, baptisms and funerals. This coincides with the fact that many clerics appear to be progressively more immersed in material matters, including politics, and are veering away from their rightful territory. This was anticipated by Paul in his first letter to Timothy: 'The Spirit says expressly that in after times some will desert from the faith and give their minds to subversive doctrines.'

Paul then gave this advice: 'Turn a deaf ear to empty and wordly chatter and the contradictions of so-called "knowledge" for many who lay claim to it have shot far wide of the faith.'

There is certainly no shortage of contradictory 'knowledge' being spread by church leaders. Cynicism garbed as enlightened sophistication is also helping to carry the churches further from the 'intellectual cradle' of Christianity. Beliefs which were promulgated through Christ are being modernised and rationalised. They are also being jettisoned.

This erosion of the foundations of faith may well accelerate the feeling that exorcism should no longer be considered acceptable because, on the subject of demons, it is advisable to discount the Bible.

Disastrous mistakes have been made in exorcism, as they have been made in other types of treatment, but it is still a greatly needed form of spiritual surgery. It would be a tragedy if those in authority were to throw away the knife.

Index

Abraham, Leon (*see also* victims) 134–6
Abraham, Patricia 134–5
American Society for Psychical Research 183
Amityville 2 (film) 138
'ancestor infestation' 119–20
animal spirits, possibility of intrusion by 183–5
anorexia nervosa, exorcism as treatment 116, 118
Anson, Canon Harold 74
apparitions 25, 28–9, 33–4, 63–7, 92, 97, 114, 117, 131, 174–80; imprint sightings: general 100–5, Carlisle 105, Central Middlesex Hospital 103–4, Charmouth, Dorset 105, Colyton, Devon 100–1, Exeter Prison 103–4, Henley, Thames Valley 103, Westminster Abbey 103–4
Australia, aboriginal magic 39–40

Baal Shem, Specialist Masters of the Divine Name 162
Badawi, Prof. Zaki 160–1
Baker, Geoffrey 146–9
Baptists 100; attitudes to exorcism 166
Barnsley, Yorkshire 143, 145
Birmingham 16, 37, 106, 179
Blatty, William Peter 136, 138
Book of the Law, The (Aleister Crowley) 49
Booth, Kay 100–3
Boston Society for Psychical Research 183
Bournemouth 86, 88, 89–91
Bowden, Father William 137
British Medical Association 110
Broadmoor (*see also* special hospitals) 109–22, 149–50
Brown, Rt. Revd David 159, 172–3
Brunswick, Father Robert 43, 77–9
Buess, Bob (*Setting the Captives Free*) 127
Burden family 86–91, 180–1, 185

cabbala, the 28, 161
Carlisle 18, 97–8, 105
Catholic Herald 120
Catholic Truth Society 138
Caulfield, Mr Justice 149
charismatic movement, attitude to exorcism 150
Cecil, Lord William Gascoyne 73
'check-list' for occult contamination 141–3
Church Army 43,77
Church of England, attitudes to exorcism 155, 156–60, 172–3
Church of God in Christ through the Holy Spirit Inc. 132
clairvoyance 13–4, 26, 74–5, 122–3
Clare, Father Arnold 9, 13–15, 20–6, 101, 174–5
Clarke, Judge Edward 47
Coggan, Dr Donald 158–9
coldness 17, 76, 86–7, 93, 182
'cone of power' 50
'contamination' by physical contact 98–9
Crowley, Aleister ('The Beast') 44, 49
Cunningham, Leon 128–31
Cupitt, Revd Don 15
curses 31–7, 38–42, 44, 46–8, 115

Daily Mirror 56
Daily Telegraph 88
demonic transference 34, 56
Devil's Prayer Book, The 71
Devils of Loudun, The 183
djinn 160–1
Dover-Wellman, Revd J. 20, 25
drugs 21–2, 27, 38, 90, 114
dybbuk 161, 163, 165

Edmonton, London 151–2
Eggins, John 145, 148
Encyclopaedia Britannica 89, 101
102
etheric screen 101–2
Exeter 9, 63, 64, 123, 176
Bishop's Commission 156–5, 159
Exorcist, The (book/film) 136–8
Expository Times, The 119–20

Faraday, Michael 102
Farm Street Church, London 75
Freud, Sigmund 107
Fromer, Jacob 162–4

Gawber, Yorkshire 145, 146
Gemmell, Jimmy 18–20, 97–100, 105
Georgetown University Medical Centre 137
gilgul (transmigration of souls) 162
Gill, Dr David 120
Giovene, Laurence 47
Glanville, Dr Terry 105
glossolalia (*see* tongues, speaking in)
Gloucester, Diocese of 8
guidelines, rites or rules regarding exorcism: Church of England 158; Methodist 166–7; Roman Catholic 35–6, 138, 140, 167–71, 176–7
Guildford, Bishop of (*see* David Brown)
Gurney, Dr Ted 109
Guy, Right Revd Basil 17

Hall, Goldie 131–2, 135
Hall, Stephanie (*see also* victims) 132, 135
Hampstead, London 20, 31
Hazlewood, Father Ian 8, 17–18, 39–40, 43–4, 85–6, 97, 125
healers/healing 14–15, 26–8, 83, 89, 114–15
healing-prayer groups 50
Health, Department of 110–12
Hebrews 28, 160–5
Hemel Hempstead 181
Homer 23
House Church Movement 53
Huxley, Aldous (*The Devils of Loudun*) 183
Hyde Park, London 151, 152

Irons, Captain Barry 43
Isis (Egyptian goddess) 45
Islamic Cultural Centre, London 160

James, Donald 147, 148
Jasper, Arkansas 131, 135
Jews (*see* Hebrews)
Josephus 161–2
juniper, use of 23–4

Kennedy, President John F. 128
Kidderminster 106
Kingston upon Thames 108
Klingenberg, Bavaria 138
Koran, the 161

Lambeth Palace 74
Lancet, The 118
Lang, Dr Cosmo 74
laurel, use of 24
Leeds Crown Court 146, 149
Liberal Catholics 9, 70, 173
Liverpool 43, 77
Lock, Ken 109
Longford, Lord 108
Loudun, France, Ursuline Convent 183
Luton, Bedfordshire 44
Lyndhurst, Hampshire 115

McAll, Dr Frances 115
McAll, Dr Kenneth 114–20, 182
MacInnes, Revd David 16–17, 37–8
Mackarness, Dr Richard 113–15, 182
McKinnon, Judge Neil 47

magic, magicians 31, 37, 39, 43–6, 48–52, 113–14, 181–2
Marriott, David 44–6, 48, 50–2
Mary Magdala 175
Matlock Bath, Derbyshire 54–5
Matthew Trust, the 108–9, 110, 180
Matthews, Dean of St Paul's 74
Medical Ethics, Journal of 15, 106
Mental Health Act (1959) 109, 149
mental health reform (*see* the Matthew Trust)
Methodist attitudes to exorcism 166, guidelines 166–7
Michel, Anneliese (*see also* victims) 139–40
Milne, Dr Hugo 149
Moniz, Egas 172
Montgomery, Alabama 132
Montgomery, Lord 108
Moslems 160–1, 165
Moss-Side (*see also* special hospitals) 110
mourning as an aid to exorcism 116–17
Myers, Eric 26–30, 175

Neil-Smith, Revd Christopher 32–7, 40–2, 155
Newton, Sir Isaac 102
New York 134–5
Norris, Demiko (*see also* victims) 132

Obsessive Poisoner (Winifred Young) 181–2
Oliver, Dr Fred 88
Omand, Revd Dr Donald 105
Oriental Templars, Ancient Order of 45
Ossett, Yorkshire 143
Ouija 53–72, 113, 117

'pact with demon' 45
Paracelsus, Trident of 45
Park Lane (*see also* special hospitals) 110
Parkinson, Preb. John 160
Pearce-Higgins, Canon John 54
Petitpierre, Dom Robert 31, 157
'placebo' exorcisms 182–3
Plato 23
Plymouth 64
Practitioner, The 113
prediction of death 58–9
polluted localities, Roman Catholic rite for exorcism 170–1
poltergeists and young people 88–9
Pope Paul VI 167
Price, Tudor 154
Prince, Dr Walter Franklin 183
protection prayer (St Patrick's Breastplate) 39
Psychic News 71

Rabinowicz, Rabbi Dr Harry 165
Rampton (*see also* special hospitals) 110
Ramsey, the Most Revd Michael 157–8
Reeves, Father Brian 176
Riggs, Ted 89
roads 'haunted' 104–5
Roman Catholic Rules 35–6, 138, 140, 167–71, 176–7
Robertson, Dr Sandy 106, 156
Robinson, Marie 143–7
Runcie, Dr Robert 157, 172
Rutherford, Beatrix (*see also* victims) 151–4

St Albans Crown Court 181
St Louis, Collegiate Church of 137
salt, use of 22–5
Scotland, Church of, attitude to exorcism 166–7
Setting the Captives Free (Bob Buess) 127
sexual assaults by psychic forces 32–7, 55–6
shadowed by the dead 81, 85–6, 90–1, 116–17
Shining, The (film) 179
Shrewsbury 97
Sidmouth, Devon 79, 81
smells 17, 24, 28, 61, 77, 95–9, 128
Smith, Mr Justice 154–5
Smith, Revd Michael 109
Smith, Revd Raymond and his wife 146–8
Solomon 162
Song, Revd James 16, 54–63
Southwark, London 54, 74

special hospitals: Broadmoor 7, 109–12, 149–50; Moss-Side 110; Park Lane 110; Rampton 110
stigmata 137
Stockwood, Dr Mervyn 74
Strover, Anthony 152–4

Tarleton, Revd George 53–4, 274–5
Taylor, Michael and Christine 143–50, 158
Thomas, the doubting disciple 175
Thompson, Peter 108–12, 180–1
tongues, speaking in 109, 144–5, 150–1
Tracy, Father John 75–6, 167
Trethowan, Professor Sir William 106–7

Underhill, Rt. Revd Francis 74

Variety 136
victims of lethal 'exorcisms': Abraham Leon 134–6; Hall, Stephanie 132–5; Michel, Anneliese 139–40; Norris, Demiko 132; Rutherford, Beatrix 151–4; Weilbacher, David 128–31
Victoria, London 151
Vincent, Revd Peter 145–7, 150

Wakefield, Yorkshire 158–9
Walters, Preb. Egerton 97
Wandsworth, London 151
Washington DC 136
Weilbacher, David (*see also* victims) 128–31
Weilbacher, Debra 128–31
Westminster Abbey 102–4, 121
Wheaton, Father John 9–14, 70, 84, 91–3, 95–6, 123–4, 173
Whittingdon, Dr Richard 179–80
Wickenden family 179–80
Willcox, Basil 88
Willesden, London 181
witches, witchcraft 31, 37–8, 41–3, 50–2, 71–2, 115, 123
Woking, Surrey 16
Worthing, Sussex 120

Yakima, Washington 128, 131
Yorkshire Post 107–8
Young, Graham 181–2
Young, Winifred (*Obsessive Poisoner*) 181–2